SOUNDS OF LANGUAGE

readers

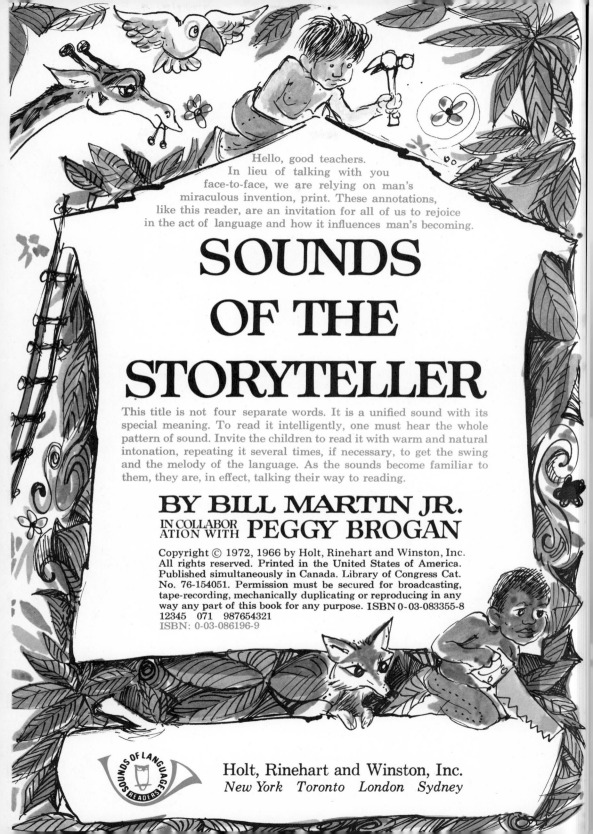

Hello, good teachers.
In lieu of talking with you
face-to-face, we are relying on man's
miraculous invention, print. These annotations,
like this reader, are an invitation for all of us to rejoice
in the act of language and how it influences man's becoming.

SOUNDS OF THE STORYTELLER

This title is not four separate words. It is a unified sound with its special meaning. To read it intelligently, one must hear the whole pattern of sound. Invite the children to read it with warm and natural intonation, repeating it several times, if necessary, to get the swing and the melody of the language. As the sounds become familiar to them, they are, in effect, talking their way to reading.

BY BILL MARTIN JR.
IN COLLABORATION WITH PEGGY BROGAN

Copyright © 1972, 1966 by Holt, Rinehart and Winston, Inc. All rights reserved. Printed in the United States of America. Published simultaneously in Canada. Library of Congress Cat. No. 76-154051. Permission must be secured for broadcasting, tape-recording, mechanically duplicating or reproducing in any way any part of this book for any purpose. ISBN 0-03-083355-8
12345 071 987654321
ISBN: 0-03-086196-9

Holt, Rinehart and Winston, Inc.
New York Toronto London Sydney

SOUNDS OF LANGUAGE READERS

The SOUNDS OF LANGUAGE program is designed to enhance a child's use of language as a speaker, a listener, a writer and a reader, and to give you teachers both the opportunities and the skills for bringing dimensions into the teaching of reading that conventional programs have precluded.

Our essay at the back of this book and the page-by-page annotations are not prescrip-

The Author and Holt, Rinehart and Winston, Inc. thank the following authors and publishers, whose help and permissions to reprint materials have made this book possible. All reasonable effort has been made to locate the source of every selection. If any errors in acknowledgments have occurred, they are inadvertent and will be corrected in subsequent editions as they are realized.

The following selections are adapted from Little Owl Books, copyright © 1963 by Holt, Rinehart and Winston, Inc., except as noted.

"Getting to Know You," "I Whistle a Happy Tune," pictures, from *Children Of The World Say "Good Morning"* by Herbert McClure. Lyrics, "Getting to Know You," "I Whistle a Happy Tune" by Oscar Hammerstein II, from THE KING AND I copyright 1951 by Richard Rodgers and Oscar Hammerstein II. Used by permission of the publishers, Williamson Music, Inc., New York, New York and Chappell & Co., Ltd.

"The Kind of Bath for Me," picture, from *The Sun Is A Star* by Sune Engelbrektson.

The following selections are adapted from Young Owl Books, copyright © 1964 by Holt, Rinehart and Winston, Inc., except as noted.

"Counting Lightly," from *Counting Lightly* by Leonard Simon.

"If You Should Meet a Crocodile," picture, from *Eleven And Three Are Poetry* compiled by Sally Nohelty.

tive. Nor are they ritual. They offer you up-to-date information about language, about human growth and about classroom organization. They offer a view of the classroom as a launching pad to human greatness, both yours and the children's.

The pupil texts are a collection of stories, poems, songs, essays, pictures and paintings that celebrate the human yen for beauty, excitement, drama, well-being and pleasure. Once you have a rich familiarity with your and the children's materials in the SOUNDS OF LANGUAGE program, you will have be-

(con't next page)

come, we believe, another link in mankind's attempt to stay the chaos of an increasingly hostile world environment.

We believe you will also discover that, without becoming a slave to a teacher's guide, you can fashion day-by-day language encounters that help children claim their human heritage as successful readers.

"Little Princess Goodnight," from *Little Princess Goodnight* by Bill Martin, Jr. with woodcut illustrations by Joseph Domjan. Copyright © 1967 by Holt, Rinehart and Winston, Inc.

"Mother Meadowlark and Brother Snake," from *Mother Meadowlark And Brother Snake* by Billy Firethunder.

"Old Lucy and the Pigeons," from *Old Lucy Lindy* by Leland Jacobs.

"Paulossie," from *Paulossie, An Eskimo Boy* by Robert C. Swim.

"The Steadfast Tin Soldier," from *The Steadfast Tin Soldier* by Hans Christian Andersen, translated from the Danish by Carl Malmburg.

"Stopping by Woods on a Snowy Evening," picture, from *Poetry for Young Scientists* compiled by Leland B. Jacobs and Sally Nohelty. Poem from *The Poetry of Robert Frost*, edited by Edward Connery Lathem. Copyright 1923 by Holt, Rinehart and Winston, Inc. Copyright 1951 by Robert Frost. By permission of Holt, Rinehart and Winston, Inc., the Estate of Robert Frost and Jonathan Cape, Ltd.

Other Sources:

Addison-Wesley Publishing Company and Hamish Hamilton, Ltd. for "The Big Cheese," from *The Big Cheese,* a Young Scott Book by Miriam Schlein with pictures by Joseph Low. Copyright © 1958 by Miriam Schlein and reprinted by permission of the publishers.

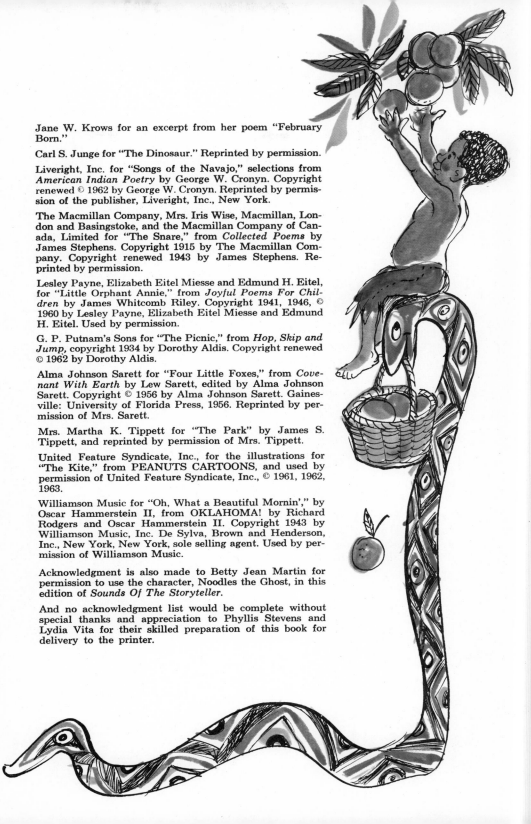

Jane W. Krows for an excerpt from her poem "February Born."

Carl S. Junge for "The Dinosaur." Reprinted by permission.

Liveright, Inc. for "Songs of the Navajo," selections from *American Indian Poetry* by George W. Cronyn. Copyright renewed © 1962 by George W. Cronyn. Reprinted by permission of the publisher, Liveright, Inc., New York.

The Macmillan Company, Mrs. Iris Wise, Macmillan, London and Basingstoke, and the Macmillan Company of Canada, Limited for "The Snare," from *Collected Poems* by James Stephens. Copyright 1915 by The Macmillan Company. Copyright renewed 1943 by James Stephens. Reprinted by permission.

Lesley Payne, Elizabeth Eitel Miesse and Edmund H. Eitel, for "Little Orphant Annie," from *Joyful Poems For Children* by James Whitcomb Riley. Copyright 1941, 1946, © 1960 by Lesley Payne, Elizabeth Eitel Miesse and Edmund H. Eitel. Used by permission.

G. P. Putnam's Sons for "The Picnic," from *Hop, Skip and Jump,* copyright 1934 by Dorothy Aldis. Copyright renewed © 1962 by Dorothy Aldis.

Alma Johnson Sarett for "Four Little Foxes," from *Covenant With Earth* by Lew Sarett, edited by Alma Johnson Sarett. Copyright © 1956 by Alma Johnson Sarett. Gainesville: University of Florida Press, 1956. Reprinted by permission of Mrs. Sarett.

Mrs. Martha K. Tippett for "The Park" by James S. Tippett, and reprinted by permission of Mrs. Tippett.

United Feature Syndicate, Inc., for the illustrations for "The Kite," from PEANUTS CARTOONS, and used by permission of United Feature Syndicate, Inc., © 1961, 1962, 1963.

Williamson Music for "Oh, What a Beautiful Mornin'," by Oscar Hammerstein II, from OKLAHOMA! by Richard Rodgers and Oscar Hammerstein II. Copyright 1943 by Williamson Music, Inc. De Sylva, Brown and Henderson, Inc., New York, New York, sole selling agent. Used by permission of Williamson Music.

Acknowledgment is also made to Betty Jean Martin for permission to use the character, Noodles the Ghost, in this edition of *Sounds Of The Storyteller*.

And no acknowledgment list would be complete without special thanks and appreciation to Phyllis Stevens and Lydia Vita for their skilled preparation of this book for delivery to the printer.

The blue-starred selections are adaptations of *Little Owl* or *Young Owl* books which significantly complement the SOUNDS OF LANGUAGE readers. Children will enjoy and profit by comparing the two versions of a story—and you will have an independent reading program operating simultaneously with your group reading program.

CONTENTS

SNIFF
SNIFF

You may be wondering about our system for annotating this book. Actually, we have tried to make the kinds of markings we think you would make as you read the essay and plan ways for making the stories and poems most enjoyable and useful for yourself and the children. Our markings are by no means complete. They are a starter, and we hope you will take pen in hand and continue the kinds of annotations that work best for you.

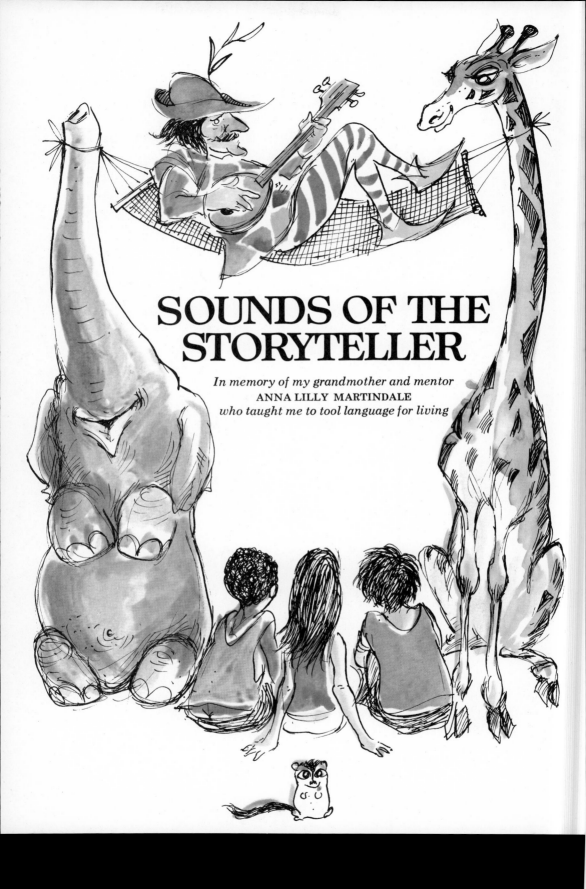

SOUNDS OF THE STORYTELLER

In memory of my grandmother and mentor
ANNA LILLY MARTINDALE
who taught me to tool language for living

Cassette recordings of Bill Martin's readings and interpretations and skill-building activities are now available with the *Sounds of Language* program. He is assisted in the recordings by the renowned guitarist, Al Caiola, who weaves musical underpinnings to the language, and by Noodles, a little ghost, who represents a child's point of view. The purpose of the recordings is to add joy and enlightenment to the reading process.

Wake up! Wake up! Come, sleeply butterfly, please join me on my journey.

As you encounter innovative arrangements of type in this book, you may be surprised at how confidently your children are willing to attack such pages. We adults have grown accustomed to school books where the same size and style of type move relentlessly from left to right, page after page, and it is easy to forget that today's children are encountering imaginative and flamboyant uses of type on T.V., in magazine advertising and even on their cereal boxes. How appropriate that school books too can call upon imaginative and intriguing page design in an effort to bring new dimensions to the children's linguistic learnings and to convince today's young readers that there is much that is alive and gripping between the covers of a book.

a haiku by Basho, painting by Charles Brey, lettering by Ray Barber

16

This delightfully nonsensical story is meant to be enjoyed and chuckled over. And isn't chuckling one nice way to explore meanings? After the children have read the story silently, you might like to invite them to read aloud some of their favorite passages. And on each rainy day when you're looking for something kind of special to do, why not read Old Lucy once again. Each re-reading will further the original pleasure found in the story.

★Old Lucy and The Pigeons

Alone rhymes with *stone* but what about *one*? Vagaries like this are part of the joy of the English language.

Old Lucy Lindy lived **alone.**

She lived alone in an old <u>stone</u> house.

The old house had an old <u>yard.</u>

Around the old yard was an old fence.

Old Lucy Lindy lived alone.

So she talked to herself.

"My!" she said to herself.

"My, my!"

Now, Old Lucy Lindy liked to live alone.

She didn't like dogs.

She didn't like cats.

And *especially* she didn't like pigeons.

"My!" said Old Lucy Lindy to herself.

"I don't like pigeons."

But pigeons came to Lucy Lindy's old house.

They came to her yard.

They came to her fence.

The pigeons   house
The birds   window
The pests

From time to time we will indicate sentences for this kind of transforming. For a discussion of this basic linguistic technique, see page 75 in the essay at the back of this book.

by Leland Jacobs, pictures by Ed Renfro   17

Repetitive sentence structures such as these occur throughout the story. How charming! And how pleasurable for those children who are still struggling to become independent readers!

Every day Old Lucy Lindy said,

"Go away, pigeons.

Go away from my fence.

Go away from my yard.

Go away from my house."

But every day the pigeons came back.

"My!" said Lucy Lindy to herself.

"What shall I do?"   Note the structural change but the identical meanings.

One morning Old Lucy Lindy said to herself,

"I know what I'll do."

All day she was busy.

She was busy with a hammer.

She was busy with nails.

She was busy with a brush.

Old Lucy Lindy made a sign.

The sign said,   How can a sign actually *say* anything?

PIGEONS, GO AWAY !

She put the sign in the yard.

Then she went to bed.

Suddenly	school
Now	work
Later	sleep

From this point on, when we suggest vocabulary substitutions (transforming sentences), we'll not necessarily include arrows.

19

Later   home
The next day   inside
The following morning   outside

The next morning Lucy Lindy went outdoors.

"My, my!" she said to herself.

There were pigeons in the yard.

There were pigeons on the house.

There were pigeons on the fence.

There were even pigeons on the sign.

Old Lucy Lindy looked and looked.

She shook her head.

"My!" said Lucy Lindy to herself.

"What stupid pigeons.

They can't even read!"

What are some other meanings of the word *even?*

Children who have used the SOUNDS OF LANGUAGE readers in grades 1 and 2 are already familiar with Old Lucy Lindy and her illogical logic. Invite them to recall the other stories they remember, including those they themselves wrote about her. They may want to borrow *Sounds of Laughter* from a second grade to re-read "Old Lucy Lindy and Her Pies," and of course, they will enjoy the *Young Owl* book "Old Lucy Lindy" which is crammed full of Lucy's antics.

Here's a Picture for Storytelling
by George Buckett

The children will be delighted to know that Noodles is still with them. Best acquaintance with Noodles comes through listening to the cassette recordings that accompany *Sounds of Language*. The children will love him.

22

BINGO

23

a fable, illustrated by Eric Carle

24

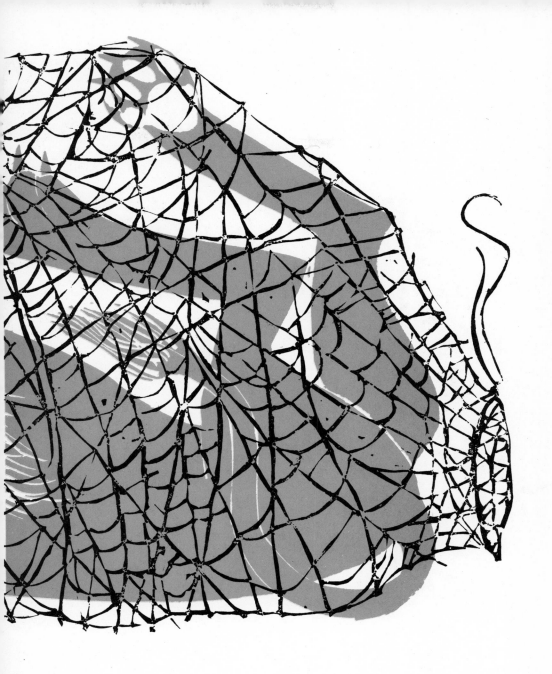

Once upon a time
a big lion was lying fast asleep in the deep woods
when a little mouse came running by.

Alas for the wee mouse!
She ran right over the mighty beast's nose!

The King of the Forest woke up with a loud roar.
He clapped his huge paw on the little mouse
and was about to gobble her down.
The tiny mouse cried pitifully:
"Please don't eat me.
Set me free,
and some day I may be able to do you a good turn."

The mighty beast smiled at the silly thought,
but he set her free.
A few days later,
the big lion,
while hunting in the woods,
fell into a trap.

He roared with a horrible sound.
The little mouse heard him
and came running fast.
She began to nibble at the stout ropes
that bound the huge beast,
and in a short time
the King of the Forest was free.

So the big lion learned
that even the littlest creatures
can be true friends in time of need.

Once upon a time
a lig bion was fying last asleep in the weep doods
when a mittle louse came bunning ry.
Alas for the mee wouse!
She ran right over the bighty neast's mose!
The Fing of the Korest woke up with a roud loar.
He clapped his puge haw on the mittle louse
and was about to dobble her gown.
The miny touse pied critifully:
"Dease plon't eat me. Fret me see,
and some day I bay me able to do you a tood gurn."

The bighty meast smiled at the thilly sought,
but he fret her see.
A dew fays later, the lig bion,
while wunting in the hoods, trell into a fap.

He roared with a sorrible hound.
The mittle louse heard him
and came funning rast.
She negan to bibble at the rout stopes
that bound the buge heast,
and in a tort shime the Fing of the Korest was free.

So the lig bion learned
that even the crittlest leatures
can be true friends in nime of teed.

What an intriguing way to discover that the beginnings of words do make a difference.

a traditional poem

The Night Before Christmas

by Clement C. Moore

'Twas the night before Christmas, when all through the house
Not a creature was stirring, not even a mouse;
The stockings were hung by the chimney with care,
In hopes that St. Nicholas soon would be there;
The children were nestled all snug in their beds,
While visions of sugar-plums danced in their heads;
And mamma in her kerchief, and I in my cap,
Had just settled our brains for a long winter nap, —
When out on the lawn there arose such a clatter,
I sprang from my bed to see what was the matter.
Away to the window I flew like a flash,
Tore open the shutters and threw up the sash.

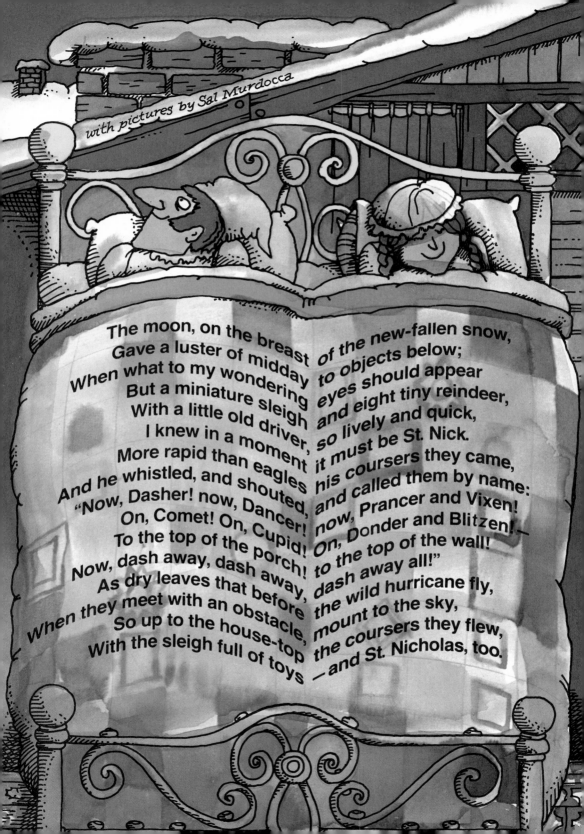

with pictures by Sal Murdocca

The moon, on the breast of the new-fallen snow,
Gave a luster of midday to objects below;
When what to my wondering eyes should appear
But a miniature sleigh and eight tiny reindeer,
With a little old driver, so lively and quick,
I knew in a moment it must be St. Nick.
More rapid than eagles his coursers they came,
And he whistled, and shouted, and called them by name:
"Now, Dasher! now, Dancer! now, Prancer and Vixen!
On, Comet! On, Cupid! On, Donder and Blitzen!—
To the top of the porch! to the top of the wall!
Now, dash away, dash away, dash away all!"
As dry leaves that before the wild hurricane fly,
When they meet with an obstacle, mount to the sky,
So up to the house-top the coursers they flew,
With the sleigh full of toys—and St. Nicholas, too.

And then in a twinkling I heard on the roof
The prancing and pawing of each little hoof.
As I drew in my head, and was turning around,
Down the chimney St. Nicholas came with a bound.
He was dressed all in fur from his head to his foot,
And his clothes were all tarnished with ashes and soot,
A bundle of toys he had flung on his back,
And he looked like a peddler just opening his pack.
His eyes, how they twinkled! his dimples, how merry!
His cheeks were like roses, his nose like a cherry;
His droll little mouth was drawn up like a bow,
And the beard on his chin was as white as the snow.
The stump of a pipe he held tight in his teeth,
And the smoke, it encircled his head like a wreath.
He had a broad face and a little round belly
That shook, when he laughed, like a bowl full of jelly.

He was chubby and plump — a right jolly old elf;
And I laughed when I saw him, in spite of myself.
A wink of his eye, and a twist of his head,
Soon gave me to know I had nothing to dread.
He spoke not a word, but went straight to his work,
And filled all the stockings; then turned with a jerk,
And laying his finger aside of his nose,
And giving a nod, up the chimney he rose.
He sprang to his sleigh, to his team gave a whistle,
And away they all flew like the down of a thistle;
But I heard him exclaim, ere he drove out of sight,
"Happy Christmas to all, and to all a good-night!"

The Kite

This story like "The Night Before Christmas" and other selections in the book will become, in brief time, a permanent part of children's oral-language treasury. You will hear them reciting and singing these things at random. And as some of the familiar phrases appear in the children's writing and speaking, you will have proof that they have claimed the language as their own. Don't follow a temptation to think the children are copying or plagiarizing. The intaking and reusing of model words, phrases, and sentences is the naturalistic way human beings go about perfecting their language skills.

Little more speed,—

© 1963, United Feature Syndicate, Inc.

little more rope, Little more wind, little more hope!

If you don't believe that type moves across the page, take a deep breath.

by Clark Gesner, pictures by Charles M. Schultz, lettering by Ray Barber

Gotta get this stupid kite to fly. Gotta make sure it doesn't drag, doesn't drag, doesn't snag, doesn't...

Gotta watch out for ev'ry little thing of

How do the children like the author's use of the word *gotta*? Perhaps they have other home-rooted expressions they'd like to experiment with. For a discussion of the importance of home-rooted language see p.120 of the essay at the back of this book.

Little less speed, little more tac, Little less rise, little more slack. Gotta keep my aim slow now... Gotta make sure it doesn't get the best of me til I get it in the air somehow!

Love it to me to have the one fool kite who likes to see a little kid cry. Millions of little kids do it ev'ry day. They make a kite, and "Look," it's in the sky.

Wow!

Little less talk, little more will, Little less luck, little more skill, Gotta face this fellow eye to eye.

Little less talk is really a reduced expression. But it doesn't seem necessary to say, "Let's have a little less talk." Now, does it?

Now that I've seen you chasing 'climbing trees, digging holes,' Wrapping your string on a 'passing fly,' why not fly?

39

Look at that, it's caught the breeze now, it's past the trees now

Wait a minute, What's it doing? —

...It isn't in the air...

with room to spare...

It isn't in a tree. It isn't on the ground. It isn't on the ground.

_It isn't on the ground.

Oh what a beautiful sight. And I'm not such a

clumsy guy. If I really try, I can really fly a

You may wonder at the extravagant use of space allowed this story and others in the collection. In certain instances we have treated white space as part of the message, as part of the time and space through which the story moves. If this song were printed as a tight little unit, the children's reading and esthetic experiences would be diminished. The frequency with which children will ask to re-read this story confirms the fact that the number of words per page is not a significant measure of reading impact.

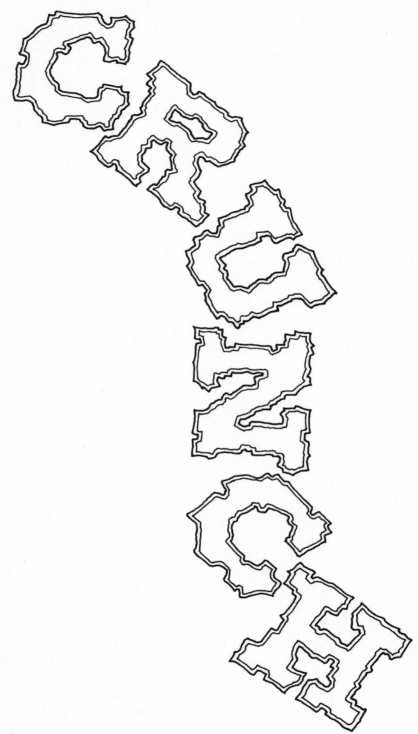

Would the children like to experiment
with words that create pictures?

Here is a catchy little tune (from "The King and I") that children can read as a poem or sing. And won't it be fun if the colorful language begins appearing in children's oral and written expression!

Getting to Know You

Getting to know all about you.

Getting to like you, getting to hope you like me,

Getting to know you, putting it my way, but nicely,

You are precisely my cup of tea!

Getting to know you, getting to feel free and easy

When I am with you, getting to know what to say.

Haven't you noticed? Suddenly I'm bright and breezy,

Because of all the beautiful and new things

I'm learning about you day by day.

by Oscar Hammerstein II

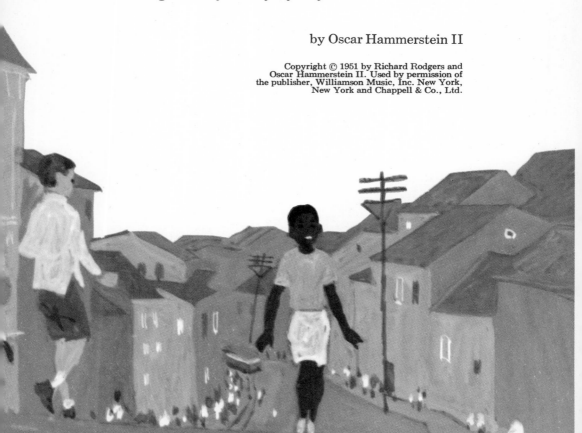

Here is another song lyric that has an intriguing rhythm and flow of language.

If you do not press for prescribed answers to the deep personal meanings that are inherent in each of these poems, you will be pleased at the quality of discussions they are apt to provoke. Above all, do not pass judgment on what a child says about his fears or his love and respect for another human being.

I Whistle a Happy Tune

Whenever I feel afraid,
I hold my head erect
And whistle a happy tune,
So no one will suspect
I'm afraid.

by Oscar Hammerstein II,
pictures by Herbert McClure

This

LA

This land is my

L

THIS is your land AND

a song by Woody Guthrie

decoration and design by Tom Huffman

Here's a productive sentence for transforming:

This	land	is	your	land.
That	house	was	my	house
	worry	will be		worry

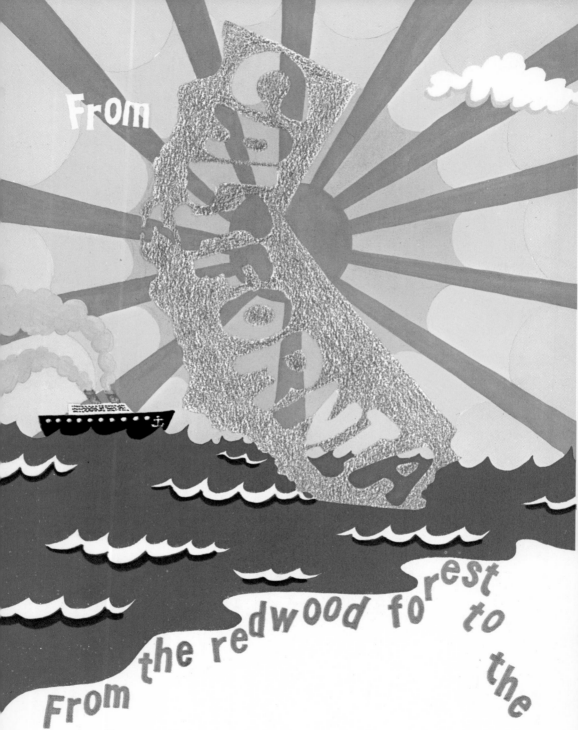

You may wish to get a recording or sheet music for this favorite Woody Guthrie melody so your class can burst into song. There isn't a nicer way to bring joy into the day. Interestingly enough, singing is also the best way to help children understand that printed language does have a rhythmical underpinning which helps to unlock its meaning.

to New York

IS LAND

WATERS

gulf stream

This land was made for

Verse 1

As I was walking that ribbon of highway
I saw above me that endless skyway
I saw below me that golden valley
This land was made for you and me.

Verse 2

I've roamed and rambled and I followed my footsteps
To the sparkling sands of her diamond deserts
And all around me a voice was sounding
This land was made for you and me.

Verse 3

When the sun comes shining and I was strolling
And the wheatfields waving and the dust clouds rolling
As the fog was lifting a voice was chanting
This land was made for you and me.

Little Orphant Annie

by James Whitcomb Riley,
pictures by Ken Longtemps

Little Orphant Annie's
   come to our house to stay,
An' wash the cups and saucers up,
   an' brush the crumbs away,
An' shoo the chickens off the porch,
   an' dust the hearth, an' sweep,
An' make the fire, an' bake the bread,
   an' earn her board-an'-keep;
An' all us other children, when the
   supper things is done,
We set around the kitchen fire
   an' has the mostest fun

See how many interesting words the children can find in this story for their word-card collection.

A-list'nin' to the witch tales 'at Annie tells about,
An' the Gobble-uns 'at gits you
      Ef you   Don't   Watch   Out!

Here is a classic poem that respects home-rooted language. Isn't it strange that we teachers can appreciate the misspellings, and the colloquialisms, and downright grammatical errors that appear in a piece of literature like this, but we find it extremely difficult to accord the same respect to the verbal and written outpourings of a child in our classrooms? If this poem serves its greatest purpose as part of the content of this reading program, it must help you, the teacher, enjoy the glories and the vagaries of children's home-rooted expressions and their struggles with spelling the language. I've never known a child yet who couldn't express himself if we adults only had the faith and the patience to listen. It takes the better part of a lifetime for the average individual to learn the ins-and-outs of our language. By our appreciation of a child's efforts and our patient faith in his power to eventually become skillful in the use of language, we may be serving our greatest roles as teachers.

Onc't they was a little boy
  wouldn't say his prayers,—
So when he went to bed at night,
  away upstairs,
His Mammy heerd him hollar,
  an' his Daddy heerd him bawl,
An' when they turn't the kivvers down,
  he wasn't there at all!

An' they seeked him in the rafter room,
  an' cubbyhole, an press,
An' seeked him up the chimbly flue,
  an' ever'wheres, I guess;
But all they ever found was thist his pants
  an' roundabout:—
An' the Gobble-uns 'll git you

Here is a favorite bit of childhood poetry that children will learn quickly just by listening to **Ef you** you reading it aloud. They will enjoy hearing it **Don't** and saying it—and eventually reading it—over and over again. Don't press children to read it until they **Watch** overtly indicate they are ready to. Once the sentences are ringing surely in their ears, you'll see them poring **Out!** over these pages, mouthing the sentences and studying the words. Even after they can read it on their own, you will want to continue using the poem as a choral-speaking selection, perhaps with everyone saying the first and last verses, the boys the second verse, and the girls the third verse.

An' one time a little girl 'ud allus laugh an' grin,
An' make fun of ever'one,
   an' all her blood an' kin;
An' onc't, when they was "company,"
   an' ole folks was there,
She mocked 'em an' shocked 'em,
   an' said she didn't care!
An' thist as she kicked her heels,
   an' turn't to run an' hide,
They was two great big Black Things
   a-standin' by her side,
An' they snatched her through the ceilin'
   'fore she knowed what she's about!
An' the Gobble-uns 'll git you

       Ef you

         Don't

           Watch

             Out!

An' little Orphant Annie says,
   when the blaze is blue,
An' the lamp-wick sputters,
   an' the wind goes woo-oo!
An' you hear the crickets quit,
   an' the moon is gray,
An' the lightnin' bugs in dew
   is all squenched away,—
You better mind yer parents, and yer teachers
   fond an' dear,
An' churish them 'at loves you,
   an' dry the orphant's tear,
Er the Gobble-uns 'll git you

                    Ef you

                         Don't

                              Watch

         Out!

abstract painting by Humphreys

What fun it would be to introduce this poem through a recording of this memorable song from the show *Oklahoma!* Then when children finally discover this portion of the song in their readers, they will hear music as they read it (or will they be singing their reading lesson?). And won't they enjoy seeing the printed form of this very familiar language!

Notice that the type has been designed to create the feeling of melody and rhythm.

Reducing sentences. From time to time we cross out describing words or whole phrases and clauses to indicate ways for reducing ornate sentences. For a discussion of the importance of this linguistic manipulation, see page 86 of the essay at the back of this book.

There's a bright golden haze

on the meadow,

There's a ~~bright~~ golden haze

Reducing

on the meadow,   *Sentences*

The corn is as high

as an elephant's eye,

An' it looks like it's climbing

clear up to the sky.

Oh, What a Beautiful Mornin'

Oh, what a beautiful day,

I got a beautiful feelin'

I got *an awful* feelin'

Everything's going my way.

Nothing's going my way

by Oscar Hammerstein II

The literary structure of this story has been annotated from page to page so that children can gain a greater appreciation of the structure of a folktale. This not only heightens their capacity to appreciate the story, but it also provides a framework within which they are more resourceful in unlocking unknown words, simply because they catch on to how the author put his story together.

★Mother Meadowlark and Brother Snake

by Billy Firethunder,
pictures by John Peterson

early
suddenly
Mother Meadowlark awakened ∧ one morning

Here is
the story
problem!!! to find a big snake curled around her nest.

Mother Meadowlark was frightened

but she spoke calmly.

kept calm
stayed calm
was calm

Frequently we will use this mark ∧ to indicate that we are expanding a sentence by adding single words or phrases and clauses. For a discussion of the importance of helping children expand sentences, see TE page 80.

"Good morning, Brother Snake,"

said Mother Meadowlark.

to know
to help "I am glad to see you.

You have not come to visit us for a long time,

so I will make you the best breakfast

that you have ever eaten!"

Mother Meadowlark is beginning to solve the problem.

The snake flicked his tongue

greedily
meanly and looked hungrily at Mother Meadowlark.

"But, unfortunately, Brother Snake,"

said Mother Meadowlark,

"a neighbor borrowed my big brass kettle,

just yesterday.

I will send one of my children to fetch it.

to get
to buy

Mother Meadowlark plans to save her children.

61

When he returns," said Mother Meadowlark,

"I will cook you the best breakfast

that you have ever eaten."

Now we see the depth of Mother Meadowlark's problem.

Mother Meadowlark nudged the baby birds

that were sleeping under her wings.

"Wake up, children," she said.

"Brother Snake has come to visit us."

Four little meadowlarks pushed their sleepy heads

out from under their mother's wing.

When they saw the big snake,

they were frightened but they stayed calm,

just like their mother.

Once children recognize that a story is organized around a problem, they will begin making predictions about the solution to the problem. These predictions help them unlock much of the vocabulary they encounter. For a discussion of ways for using literary structure to decode print, see page 24 of the essay at the back of this book.

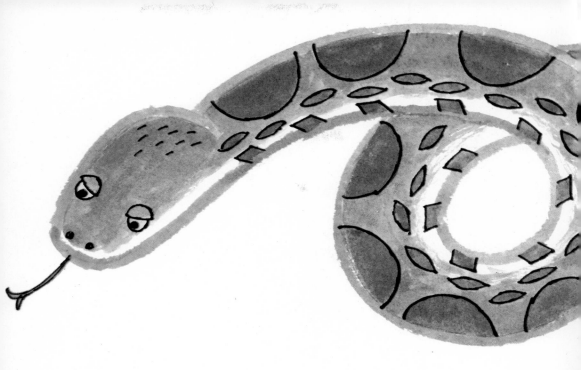

"All of my children are named after you,
Brother Snake,"
said Mother Meadowlark.
"This is my first child.
He is named Scaly-Skin.
I will send him to the neighbors
to bring back my brass kettle."

Mother Meadowlark gave the first baby bird
a little nudge.
He hopped to the edge of the nest.

for

<u>Scaly-Skin.</u> Word card

to the rim

tree
rock
limb

Mother Meadowlark flatters her
enemy to outwit him.

The baby bird
is reflecting
his mother's
cunning
in being polite
to the snake.
How did he
catch on to the
plan so quickly?

Hello
Howdy

"Good morning, Brother Snake,"

he said politely.

quietly, angrily, fearfully, shyly

The snake flicked his tongue

and looked hungrily

Here's an interesting word for the
children's word-card collection.

at the first baby bird.

"Be off now, Scaly-Skin,"

said Mother Meadowlark,

"and bring back my brass kettle."

The first baby is saved. Since there are four baby birds, we immediately hunch that this pattern of language and action will be repeated three more times in this folktale.

> Mother Meadowlark gave the first baby bird
> another little nudge,
> and he lifted his wings
> and flew quickly out of the nest.
> He landed about thirty feet away
> in the tall grass.

End of the first episode.

More
flattery.
Then Mother Meadowlark said,

"My second child is also named after you,

Brother Snake.

I call him Beady-Eyes." Word card

Mother Meadowlark gave the second baby bird

a little nudge.

He hopped to the edge of the nest.

66

Are the children noticing that the language and action are both repeating with the second baby bird?

"Good morning, Brother Snake,"
he said politely.

The snake flicked his tongue hungrily
at the second baby bird.

The action
repeats.

"I wonder what is keeping Scaly-Skin ~~so long~~,"
said Mother Meadowlark.
  "Beady Eyes,
you'd better go over there
and help him.
Maybe the brass kettle is too heavy
for him to carry."

hot
big

The second
baby bird
is saved!
Mother Meadowlark gave the second baby bird

another little nudge,

and he lifted his wings

and quickly flew out of the nest. Where is this nest?

He landed about thirty feet away

in the tall grass.

End of the second episode.

More flattery.

No sooner had he landed
than Mother Meadowlark said,
"This is my ~~third~~ child,
Brother Snake.
I also named her after you.
She is called Creep-Along."

Mother Meadowlark gave the third baby bird
a little nudge.

<u>She</u> <u>hopped</u> <u>to</u> <u>the</u> <u>edge</u> <u>of</u> <u>the</u> <u>nest.</u>

Notice how we can rearrange this basic sentence
structure and have the same meanings:

To the edge of the nest she hopped.
To the edge of the nest hopped she.

"Good morning, Brother Snake,"

she said politely.

calmly, happily, quietly, suddenly

The snake flicked his tongue

and looked ~~hungrily~~

at the third baby bird.

Are the children aware of what happens to the sentence
when it is reduced by leaving out the one word *hungrily*?

The action repeats
a third time.

Mother Meadowlark said,
"Creep-Along,
go tell the boys to hurry.
I know that my Brother
is hungry and is waiting
for his breakfast."

The third baby
is safe!

Mother Meadowlark
gave the third baby bird
another little nudge.
The third baby bird lifted her wings
and quickly flew out of the nest.
She landed in the ~~tall~~ grass
thirty feet away.

End of the
third episode.

Notice the slight variation of this sentence
from the way it appeared on page 69:
He landed about thirty feet away in the tall grass.

No sooner had she landed

than Mother Meadowlark said,

More
flattery. "I wonder what can be keeping

the children so long.

They must be playing along the way.

I should have sent No-Ears. Word card

She also is named after you,

Brother Snake.

She is the only one of my children

who usually does what she's told."

always
generally

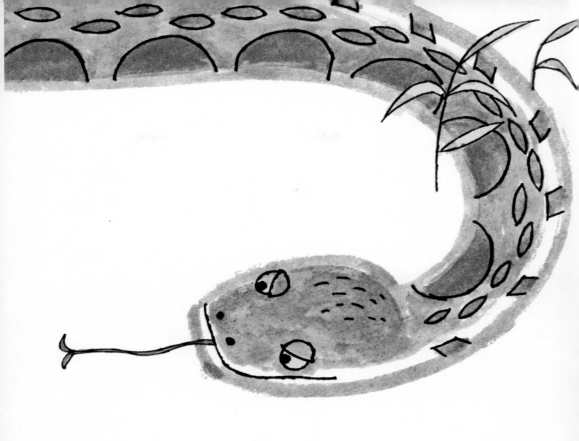

All of the children know by now that this sequence of action and these patterns of language are a basic part of the story.

Mother Meadowlark gave the fourth baby bird
a little nudge.
She hopped to the edge of the nest.
   "Good morning, Brother Snake,"
she said politely.
   The snake flicked his tongue
and looked hungrily
at the fourth baby bird.

The word *to* could be substituted here for the word *and,* and the meaning of the sentence would not be changed. Also note that the word *and* could be left out and the meaning would not be affected. Isn't our language tricky?

The action repeats a fourth time.

"No-Ears," said Mother Meadowlark, "would you go and find your brothers and sister? My Brother is hungry and wants his breakfast ~~very much indeed.~~"

How do the children feel about reducing the beautifully constructed sentences in this story?

The fourth baby
bird is saved.

Mother Meadowlark gave the fourth baby bird
another little nudge.
She lifted her wings and flew out of the nest,
into the tall grass.

End of the fourth episode.

She flew *into* the tall grass.
She landed *in* the tall grass.
Notice that in one case we must say *into*, but in the second
case we must say the word *in*. What's the difference in meaning?

Who is *she,* the baby bird or the mother?

As soon as she had left the nest,

Mother Meadowlark said,

"Farewell, Brother Snake.

You are not going to get any breakfast."

We can substitute *your* or *a* in this sentence for the word *any,* or we could leave the word *any* out altogether and the meaning would not be changed. Oh, how glorious is our language!

Notice these two nice chunks of meaning at the end of the sentence. Here are some other phrases that are triggered off by the same kind of word.

Then she, too, flew away to join her children

in the safety of the tall grass.

in the field	*of* the building
in the winter	*of* the shadow
in the meantime	*of* our class
in the park	*of* the group
	under the roof
	under the bridge
	under the wire

End of the fifth episode.

In "Mother Meadowlark and Brother Snake" we have provided both literary and skillbuilding annotations. You, the teacher, are the person to decide what kinds of post-reading discussions you want to have with children after reading a story or poem. Sometimes the children's responses might invite you to focus primarily on the author's way of putting a poem or story together. Sometimes the children may be intrigued with his way of using language or with their own exploration of meanings. Sometimes you may want simply to ask, *Well, what do you think about this?* so the children can react in their self-selected ways. And sometimes you may wish to say nothing at all—sensing that the children's response to the story or poem is complete without verbalizing.

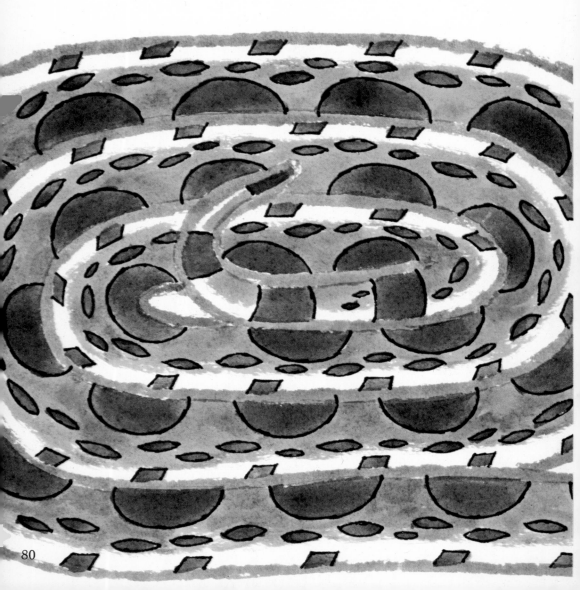

Have you noticed throughout the story how the artist, John Peterson, designed the snake on the page to help you feel his horrible presence? This is a classic example of design that fully complements a particular story.

Children, when did you begin to hunch that the same action was going to happen more than once in this story? When did you predict that certain language would be repeated? Isn't it interesting that your reading becomes easier when you figure out how an author has put his story together?

Notice how many different ways we can rearrange the chunks of meaning in the sentence without destroying the original meaning:
And . . . that night Brother Snake went home hungry.
And . . . Brother Snake went home that night hungry.
And . . . Brother Snake that night went home hungry.
But we cannot say
And . . . Brother Snake hungry that night went home.

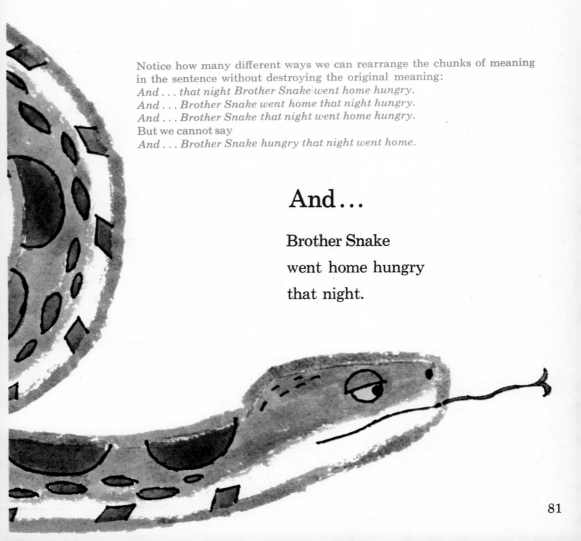

And...

Brother Snake
went home hungry
that night.

This lends itself to literary analysis since the author's structure is both intriguing and clearly seen. Can the children find her rhyme scheme? Can they discover the underlying rhythmic pattern? This kind of investigation of literary structure helps children expect structure in stories and poems and helps them do this kind of analyzing when they are reading on their own. Once they catch on to how a story or poem is put together, they can predict much of the language and have in their possession a useful word-unlocking skill.

A long man,
A strong man,
A February-born man.
A rough man, a tough man,
A cannot-learn-enough man.
A farmer and a clerk.
A statesman and a president
Who knew all kinds of work.
Read by flickering firelight
And feeble candle flame.
Born of simple parents—

Abe Lincoln was his name.

a poem "February Born" by Jane W. Krows, picture by Oscar Berger

Here's a Picture for Storytelling

by George Buckett

If your children are not acquainted with the friendly ghost Noodles, you may wish to borrow a copy of *Sounds I Remember* where Noodles first appears.

After several readings of this story, the children may wish to borrow the author's literary structure and hang their own ideas on it. Whenever children innovate on the structure of a story or a poem, they are having first-hand experience with the fact that stories and poems do have frameworks on which they are built. Gradually the children build the habit of looking for literary structure, enjoying the fact that they can predict much of the language simply by recognizing how the author hung his story or poem together. SOUNDS OF LANGUAGE helps develop this linguistic insight into word-unlocking skills. For a discussion of ways for developing these skills, see p. 24 of the essay at the back of this book.

There was a princess, a lovely princess.

Her name was Little Princess Goodnight.

*She put
her unicorn
under
her pillow.*

*She put
her dragon
under
her bed.*

She put

her peacock

under

her chair.

She put

her mouse

under

her slipper.

90

This story is illustrated with woodcuts by Joseph Domjan, whose work hangs in museums around the world. Children may enjoy comparing his art style to others in this book. The more sensitive children become, to the varied offerings of books and of the printed page, the more reading and books will become a necessary part of their lives.

And then she crept into bed

and fell asleep.

But not the mouse . . .

The mouse crept out from under the slipper
and pinched the peacock under the chair.
The peacock crept out from under the chair
and pinched the dragon under the bed.
The dragon crept out from under the bed
and pinched the unicorn under the pillow.
And the unicorn started to cry!

The little princess awakened.
"O dear!" she said.
"What shall I do?"
She thought
and she thought

and she thought.
Then...

Little princess Goodnight jumped out of bed.

She put her unicorn

on top of her pillow.

She put her dragon

on top of her bed.

She put her peacock

on top of her chair.

She put her mouse

on top of her slipper.

And she,

Little Princess Goodnight,

crept under her bed

and went back to sleep.

She was a lovely princess.

The
peacock	crept	out
teacher	peered	out
prince	flew	down
king	stormed	in
boss	rushed	in

from
under	the	chair
under	her	eyebrows
over	his	treetops
beyond	a	mountain
down		hall

Most stories and poems have sentences that are worth manipulating both for the fun and for the linguistic learnings involved. You will want to be sure that the children have enjoyed the literary selections in all of their beauty and wholeness before engaging in such followup activities. Be sure, too, that the children again hear the stories and poems in wholeness after the linguistic manipulations are over.

An integral part of the SOUNDS OF LANGUAGE program is children's active manipulation of language. This program stresses the sentence sound above word sounds, recognizing that the words within the sweep of the sentence tend to take on different meanings and overtones than when analyzed in isolation. The sentence given here is one that the children will recognize as having come from "Little Princess Goodnight."

Shown here is the technique of substituting other words for each of the key words in the sentence, thereby using the original sentence structure to express new thoughts. Throughout the program whenever you and the children come upon a sentence that you like, you may want to write the sentence on the board, and then invite the children to make vocabulary substitutions for the various words. A substitution for a given word is written directly beneath the original word. The children can then pick from each column their favorite words and spin a new sentence. This type of fun with language (transforming a sentence) invites children to speculate about the utility of a given sentence in a variety of conceptual situations. Transforming sentences also helps children appreciate the order and the function of various kinds of words in English sentences.

PUZZLE *How many different sentences can you make using this sentence for a pattern?*

and
| pinched |
| praised |
| kissed |
| slammed |
| threw |

the
| dragon |
| student |
| princess |
| door |
| inkwell |

under	the	bed.
for	his	work.
on	her	cheek.
off	its	hinges.
across	the	room.

As you read aloud to the children, leave out the last word in the poem. Chances are they will all chime in on the word *dinner,* demonstrating that they have caught on to the rhyme scheme. For a discussion of the use of rhyme scheme in word unlocking, see p. 45 of the essay at the back of this book.

If you should meet a crocodile

Don't take a stick and poke him;
Ignore the welcome in his smile,
Be careful not to stroke him.
For as he sleeps upon the Nile,
He thinner gets and thinner;
And whene'er you meet a Crocodile
He's ready for his dinner.

author unknown,
picture by Kelly Oechsli

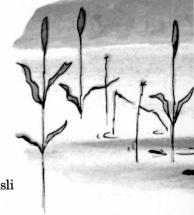

Why not give the children a break and let them determine how they best can intake the humor and joy of these two poems? It might be fun to invite them, without any supervision on your part, to divide up into groups and work out ways to do choral presentations of either or both of these verses. You may be surprised how creatively dramatic they can be in responding to the stretch of rhythmic structure.

The Dinosaur

A beast of yore,

Doesn't live here

Any more.

by Carl S. Junge,
picture by Robert Jon Antler

The King's Breakfast

by A. A. Milne,
pictures by Ernest Shepard

Here is a memorable experience in melody, rhythm, and whimsey which endears itself to all who care to listen. Your only obligation in making this a great reading experience for the children in your class is to read it aloud a good many times in practice before you attempt to read it to the children.

The basic rhythm of this poem can best be illustrated by this visual example:

All of the direct statements of the characters in this poem have been marked in blue. This is to signal you to have a good time impersonating each spokesman. Don't be afraid to let yourself go and have a good time in the reading. The essential things are to keep the poem moving rapidly and to keep your reading sincere, yet almost tongue-in-cheek. And, by the way, do you realize that you have both a high voice and a low voice that you can use in impersonating the various voices in this poem?

The King asked

The Queen, and

The Queen asked

The Dairymaid:

"Could we have some butter for

The Royal slice of bread?"

The Queen asked

The Dairymaid,

The Dairymaid

Said, "Certainly,

I'll go and tell

The cow

Now

Before she goes to bed."

The basic rhythm of this poem is *short-short*-LONG, *short-short*-LONG. The poem skips along merrily with little concern for meaning. Don't burden children with comprehension questions about this poem; just let them enjoy this music and wonder—which after all is comprehension at its best.

The Dairymaid

She curtsied,

You may wish to invite the children to clap the underlying rhythm of this poem. This is one impressive way to help children know that poems and sentences and even words have basic melodies.

And went and told

The Alderney: A British breed of cow.

"Don't forget the butter for

Make the Dairymaid sound officious.

The Royal slice of bread."

The Alderney

Said sleepily:

"You'd better tell

The cow is sleepy. You may wish to yawn along with this speech.

His Majesty

That many people nowadays

Like marmalade

Instead."

The Dairymaid
Said, "Fancy!" The Dairymaid is dead serious!
She believes what the cow has said.
And went to
Her Majesty.
She curtsied to the Queen, and
She turned a little red:
"Excuse me, She is a little embarrassed now
to tell the Queen that the butter
Your Majesty, is not forthcoming.
For taking of
The liberty,
But marmalade is tasty, if
It's very
Thickly
Spread."

The Queen said

"Oh!" | The Queen is now dead serious, as she believes there will be no butter.

And went to

His Majesty:

"Talking of the butter for

The Royal slice of bread,

Many people

Think that

Marmalade

Is nicer.

Would you like to try a little

Marmalade

Instead?" | The Queen, because she is a queen, is very firm in telling the King this bit of bad news.

The King said,

"Bother!" | The King is agitated.

And then he said,

"Oh, deary me!" | The King is provoked.

The King sobbed, "Oh, deary me!" | The King is whimpering.

And went back to bed.

"Nobody," | He's almost sobbing.

He whimpered

"Could call me

A fussy man;

I *only* want

A little bit

Of butter for

My bread!"

From the Editor: We goofed in the first printing of this book. The word *Bother!* in the fifteenth line down on this page appeared as *Brother!* But wouldn't the children have a great time analyzing the difference in these two expressions? Mr. Milne, the poet, probably wouldn't agree, however.

The Queen said,
"There, there!"

The Queen is motherly
in quieting the King.

And went to
The Dairymaid.

The Dairymaid
Said, "There, there!"
And went to the shed.

The Dairymaid is
over-anxious about
the King.

The cow said,
"There, there!
I didn't really
Mean it;
Here's milk for his porringer
And butter for his bread."

The cow is solicitous
and quite willing now
to produce the butter.

The Queen took
The butter
And brought it to
His Majesty;

The King said,

"Butter, eh?"

And bounced out of bed.

"Nobody," he said,

As he kissed her

Tenderly,

The King feels increasingly better from now on to the end of the story.

"Nobody," he said,

As he slid down

The banisters,

"Nobody,

My darling,

Could call me

A fussy man—

He sheepishly defends his emotional tirade.

BUT

I do like a little bit of butter for my bread!"

THE STEADFAST TIN SOLDIER

by Hans Christian Andersen translated by Carl Malmburg

Once upon a time there were twenty-five tin soldiers.
They were all brothers,

Note how Andersen gives a human quality to pieces of molded metal.

for they had been made from the same old tin spoon.
Each one stood stiffly at attention,
looking straight ahead and keeping his rifle shouldered.

with pictures by Michael Wood

Here is one of the great love stories of all
literature. Because the characters are toy-
like—a one-legged tin soldier and a paper
ballerina—children are able to accept their
love with no embarrassment. And make
no mistake, children think more deeply
about love than we sometimes realize.

And they all looked very smart
in their red and blue uniforms.
The very first thing they heard in this world,
when the lid was taken off their box,
was a little boy clapping his hands
and exclaiming, "Tin soldiers!"
They had been given to him as a birthday present,
and he immediately set them up on the table.

What a
beautiful
sentence
to read
aloud!

An introduction to the main character.

Each soldier looked exactly like the others,
except for one, who was just a little different.
He had only one leg,
for he had been poured into the mold last of all
and there had not been quite enough tin to finish him.
Nevertheless, he stood just as firmly on one leg
as the others did on their two,
and of all the soldiers he was the one
that people would some day hear about.

What a
difficult
sentence
to read
aloud!

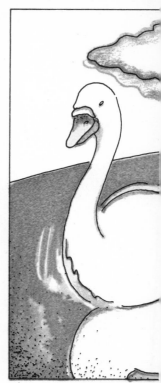

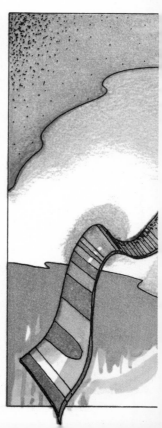

This complex sentence becomes more tenable when it is broken down into its *chunks of meaning*.

On the table there were many other toys,

but what caught the eye first

was a fine paper castle with tiny windows,

through which you could look and see the rooms inside.

Outside the castle, little trees had been placed

around a mirror which was a make-believe lake.

Wax swans floated on the surface of the mirror

and were reflected in it.

It was all very charming,

but prettiest of all was a little lady

who stood in the open doorway of the castle.

Chunks of meaning.

She too was cut out of paper,

but wore a skirt of sheerest linen,

and over her shoulder was draped a narrow blue ribbon

on which glittered a spangle as big as her face.

The little lady held both her arms outstretched,

for she was a dancer,

and she kicked one leg so high into the air

that the tin soldier could not see it.

So he thought that she, too,

had only one leg, as he did.

The story problem.

"Now, that's the very wife for me!" he thought.

"But she is a lady of high rank and lives in a castle,

whereas I have only a box,

and there are twenty-five of us sharing that.

No, that would be no place for her!

But anyway, I must try to make her acquaintance."

If the tin soldier had known that the ballerina had two legs, would he have been so quick to fall in love with her?

Then he stretched out behind a snuffbox that stood on the table. From there he could watch the charming little lady who stood on one leg without ever losing her balance. Late in the evening the other tin soldiers were put back into the box, and the people in the house went to bed. Then the toys began to play. They played paying visits, fighting battles, and giving parties. The tin soldiers rattled around in their box, for they wanted to join in the fun, but they could not lift the lid. The nutcracker turned somersaults,

Children, would you like to draw a picture of the toys at play?

Who would like to write the verse
that the canary spoke to the toys?

and the slate pencil scribbled on the slate. There was such a commotion that the canary woke up and began to join in the conversation—in verse, if you can believe such a thing! The only two who did not stir were the tin soldier and the little dancer. She remained poised on the tip of her toe with both her arms outstretched. He stood steadfastly on his one leg and did not for a moment take his eyes off her.

His plan to resolve the problem.

How long can you stand on the tip
of one foot without losing balance?

What a dramatic and interesting sentence. Notice how the word *pop* and its pronunciation heightens the drama.

Then the clock struck midnight and — pop! — up snapped the lid of the snuffbox! But there was no snuff in it — instead, there was a little goblin. It was a trick snuffbox, you see, meant to startle people. "Tin soldier," said the goblin, "you had better keep your eyes to yourself!" But the tin soldier pretended not to hear. "All right!" said the goblin. "You just wait until tomorrow!"

Here is the enemy to prevent the solution to the problem.

Could it be that the goblin too was in love with the ballerina?

Who can read this to show the meanness of the wicked goblin?

Was the goblin little or big?

Children, notice *window sill* is written as two words but has a single meaning. On the other hand, *housemaid* is two words written as one word with a single meaning.

The next morning, after the children got up, the tin soldier was moved over to the window sill. Whether what happened next was

This theme recurs at the end of the story.

the work of the goblin or a gust of wind, we do not know, but suddenly the window flew open, and the soldier fell headlong from the third story. It was a terrifying fall. He landed with his head down, his one leg up in the air, and his bayonet stuck between two paving stones. The housemaid and the little boy ran down at once to look for him,

The enemy creates the first obstacle.

Why do you suppose the soldier was too proud to ask for help?

but although they almost stepped on him, they did not see him. If the tin soldier had cried out, "Here I am!" they would surely have found him, but he did not think it was proper to shout when he was in uniform. Soon it began to rain. The raindrops fell faster and faster, until it was a regular downpour. When the storm was over, two street urchins came along. "Look!" one of them said,

"There's a tin soldier!

Let's send him for a sail."

Circumstance creates the second obstacle.

So they made a boat out of an old newspaper, and put the tin soldier inside. Away he sailed down the gutter, while the boys ran along beside him clapping their hands. Goodness, what great waves there were in the gutter, and what a swift current![1] The paper boat pitched [2]and tossed [3]and whirled so fast [4]that the tin soldier became quite dizzy. But he did not flinch or show the least sign of fear. He looked straight ahead and kept a firm hold on his rifle.

on it

Notice the chunks of meaning in this sentence.

Circumstance creates the third obstacle.

All of a sudden the boat was swept into a long drain pipe. There it was as dark as it had been in the box. "I wonder where I'm headed," the tin soldier thought. "If only I had the little lady here in the boat with me, it might be twice as dark and I shouldn't mind a bit!"

Kiss! Kiss! Wow!

Notice how placing *there* at the beginning of the sentence adds to the power of the sentence.

119

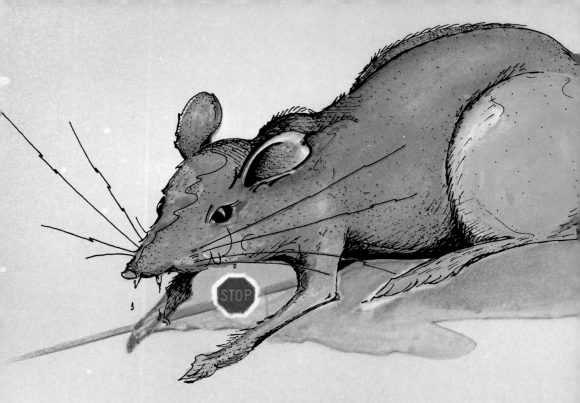

Circumstance creates the fourth obstacle.

Just at that moment there appeared a huge water rat

who lived in the pipe.

"Have you a passport?" asked the rat. "Hand it over!"

The tin soldier did not answer,

Who can read the rat's speeches to show how terrifying a rat can be?

but clasped his rifle tighter than ever.

The boat rushed on with the rat close behind it.

Oh, how he gnashed his teeth

and shouted to the sticks and straws

floating in the stream: "Stop him! Stop him! He didn't pay his toll!

He wouldn't show his passport!"

Notice the punctuation.

The current grew swifter and swifter.

Now the tin soldier could see daylight ahead,

but he heard a roaring noise

that was enough to frighten even the bravest of men.

Just think! Where the pipe ended,

the water emptied into a big canal.

The tin soldier felt as frightened

as you and I would if we were about

to be swept over a huge waterfall.

But now he was so close to the edge

that he could not escape.

The boat shot out into the canal,

while the tin soldier held himself as straight as he could—

nobody could say of him that he had

so much as blinked an eye.

The boat spun around three or four times

and filled with water to the brim.

It was sure to sink.

to collapse, to ride out the storm, to flounder in the waves

The tin soldier soon stood in water up to his neck,

and the boat sank deeper and deeper.

Circumstance creates the fifth obstacle.

Now the paper began to come apart.

The soldier felt the water swirling about his head,

and as he went under he thought

of the lovely little dancer whom he would never see again.

In his ears rang the words of an old song:

"ONWARD! DANGER CALLS YOU, SOLDIER!

DEATH AWAITS YOU IN THE FIELD!"

Who can make up a tune for singing this song?
Maybe you would like to add some lines of your own to the song.

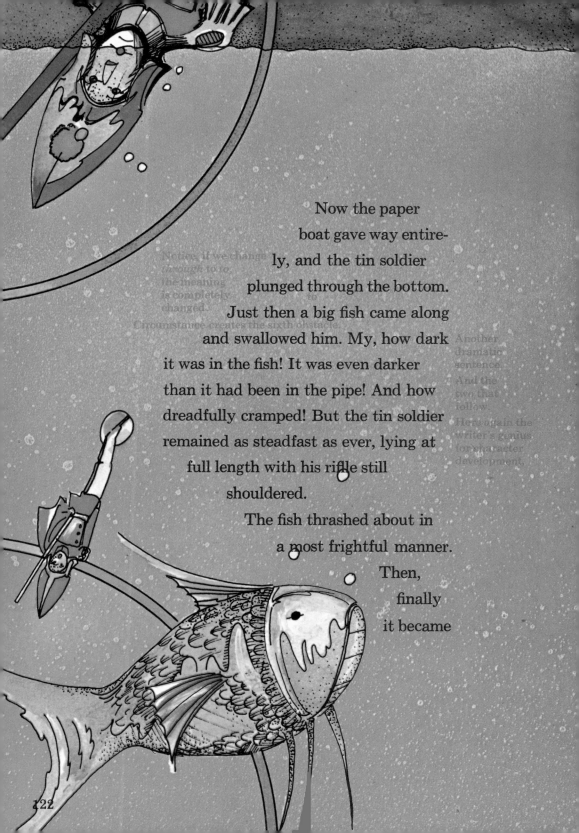

Now the paper
boat gave way entire-
ly, and the tin soldier
plunged through the bottom.
Just then a big fish came along
and swallowed him. My, how dark
it was in the fish! It was even darker
than it had been in the pipe! And how
dreadfully cramped! But the tin soldier
remained as steadfast as ever, lying at
full length with his rifle still
shouldered.
The fish thrashed about in
a most frightful manner.
Then,
finally
it became

Notice, if we change
through to *to,*
the meaning
is completely
changed.

Circumstance creates the sixth obstacle.

Another
dramatic
sentence.
And the
two that
follow.
Here again the
writer's genius
for character
development.

very quiet. After some
time, a flash of lightening
seemed to penetrate the
darkness. Suddenly it was
daylight again, and someone
exclaimed, "A tin soldier!" The fish had
been caught, taken to the market and
sold, and was now in the kitchen where
the maid had just cut it open with a big
knife. She picked the tin soldier up by
the waist, and with two fingers
carried him into the living room.
Everyone was eager to get a look
at such a remarkable fellow—
a tin soldier who had
traveled around in the
belly of a fish!

Ah! The fish was
caught! How lucky
for the soldier!

Can a good soldier ever be vain?

But the tin soldier did not let their admiration
go to his head.

Here is another beautifully dramatic sentence.
They set him up on the table, and then

—what strange things do happen in this world!—

he found he was in the very same room

*The hope builds
by circumstance.* that he had been in before.

He saw the very same children.

The very same toys stood on the table—

there was the splendid castle,

and the lovely little dancer.

She was still standing poised on one leg

with the other high in the air.

*Now he knows
that the ballerina* Yes, she was steadfast, too.
loves him!

The tin soldier was so deeply moved

that he almost shed tin tears,

but that of course was something

a soldier could never do.

So he gazed at her and she gazed at him,

but neither of them said a word.

*Children, there are many good
words in this story for your
word cards.*

At that moment, for no reason at all,

the little boy picked up the tin soldier

and threw him into the fireplace.

But, alas! The enemy returns. The danger still exists!

Without doubt,

it was the goblin in the snuffbox

who was to blame for it.

The tin soldier stood there lit up by the flames.

He began to feel terribly hot,

but whether the heat came from the fire,

or from the love burning within him,

he did not know.

Oh, how swiftly comes this bad turn of events! The story races toward its climax.

The bright colors were gone from his uniform;

whether because of all he had been through

or because of grief, who can tell?

He gazed at the little lady and she gazed at him.

He felt himself melting away,

but he remained steadfast,

standing at attention,

shouldering his rifle.

The forewarning of death becomes reality. The enemy seems to have won.

Notice how frequently Andersen likened the characteristics of a molded tin soldier to qualities of human greatness.

But no! By circumstance—and steadfast-
ness—the soldier and his love are at last
united . . . just as he wishes they would
be. The story ends triumphantly.

Could it be that the ballerina herself chose to die with
her sweetheart? The death of lovers is a subject of
many great legends and operas. *Aida* is one.

Suddenly a door was opened.

A gust of wind caught the little dancer,

and, like a sylph, she fluttered into the fire

and landed right next to the tin soldier.

She burst into flame and was gone!

The tin soldier melted down to a lump,

and the next day,

when the housemaid emptied the ashes,

she found him in the shape of a little tin heart.

But all that was left of the dancer

was her spangle,

and that was burnt black as coal.

There may be some children who will weep as they respond to this tenderly strong story. Your objective attitudes will help such children accept
their fears as a natural response to literary experience, and it will help the
dry-eyed children know that there is nothing wrong with shedding tears.
After all, can we really say that the person who involves himself in an
emotional story without showing his feelings is any better or lesser than a
person who weeps? Our culture has made a fetish of equating tears with
weakness. How ridiculous!

The effect of this poem is the beat of the drums that one hears during a parade. The beat of the drum is very regular—those beats have been indicated by the lines under the appropriate syllables. The rhythm is *short*-LONG-*short*-*short*-LONG.

A Parade

A parade!   A parade!

A-rum-a-tee-tum

I know a parade

By the sound of the drum.

    A-rum-a-tee-tum

    A-rum-a-tee-tum

    A-rum-a-tee-tum-

    a-tee-tum.

Here it comes.

Down the street.

I know a parade

By the sound of the feet.

Music and feet

Music and feet

Can't you feel

The sound and the beat?

    A-rum-a-tee-tum

    A-rum-a-tee-tum

    A-rum-a-tee-tum-

    a-tee-tum.

by Mary Catherine Rose

Both of the poems here lend themselves to choral reading and choral speaking. After reading the poems aloud several times, the children will tend to know them, and you can start building a repertoire of poems that can be recited by memory. What a delightful way to come to love both poetry and language!

Here is a homey little poem that tickles the funny bone and makes poetry immediately available to children.

The Picnic

We brought a rug for sitting on,

Our lunch was in a box.

The sand was warm. We didn't wear

Hats or Shoes or Socks. How can such varied spellings have similar sounds? Wouldn't *sox* be fun for *socks*?

Waves came curling up the beach.

We waded. It was fun.

Our sandwiches were different kinds.

I ~~my jelly~~ one.

dropped

by Dorothy Aldis

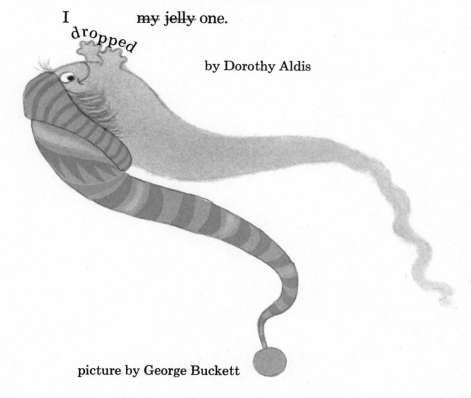

picture by George Buckett

Noodles

and the

MAIL BOX

A CONVERSATION THAT COULD BE ACTED OUT

(MUSIC DOWN-START SCENE)

Bill: Noodles! What are you doing in my mailbox?

Noodles: Oh, I'm just resting in here. Hello! Hello there, Bill Martin.

Bill: Any mail in there for me today?

Noodles: Yes, but it wasn't very interesting. Just three Christmas cards.

Bill: You've been reading my mail.

Noodles: I didn't get any, so I read yours.

Bill: Well, maybe you didn't write any letters. You know, you don't get letters if you don't write any.

Here is a typical Bill Martin—Noodles conversation like those on the SOUNDS
OF LANGUAGE tapes. What fun for the children to play the roles!

Noodles: Well, come to think of it, I just forgot to mail my Christmas cards this year.

Bill: You did? Well, no wonder you didn't get any.

Noodles: Do you think it's too late to send them now?

Bill: Well, yes. It's Christmas Eve.

Noodles: Oh, well. Say, I'll sing my Christmas greetings right now. Suppose that'll be all right?

Bill: Well, I-I'm sure all your friends are listening. They would like to hear you.

Noodles: Oh, but-- only, I can't sing.

Bill: Of course you can. Everyone can sing.

Noodles: Oh-ho, you don't know. Well, sound your "do." Do-do. Re-re. Mi-mi. Hey, would you help me?

(He pulls Bill near to whisper in his ear.)

Bill: Well, if I could. O-oh! Don't bite me!

Noodles: Ehh--Come here, come here.

Bill: What?

Noodles: Well, don't sing too loud, will you?

Bill: No, I won't sing too loud. Boys and girls, Noodles wants to sing you his Christmas greetings, which he forgot to mail.

(MUSIC)

Noodles and Bill:
We wish you a Merry Christmas,
We wish you a Merry Christmas,
We wish you a Merry Christmas,
And a Happy New Year.

Oh, bring us some figgy pudding,
Oh, bring us some figgy pudding,
Oh, bring us some figgy pudding,
And bring some out here.

We won't go until we get some,
   We won't go until we get some,
We won't go until we get some,
   So bring some out here.

We wish you a Merry Christmas,
   We wish you a Merry Christmas,
We wish you a Merry Christmas,
   And a Happy New Year.

Noodles: *A very, very, very Happy New Year!*
   (END OF SONG)

Noodles: Oh, beautiful, beautiful. Only you sang too loud.

Bill: Oh, Noodles.

Noodles: Well, I have such a lovely voice, don't I?

Bill: Yes, Noodles, you do.

Noodles: I'm going now and start addressing my Christmas cards for next year.

Noodles: Good-bye, Bill. Oodely, oodely!

Bill: Good-bye, Noodles. Oh, just a moment. Can you come over to the Wish Shop for a story? I'm going to tell a story in a moment.

Noodles: No, no, I'm too busy. But, uh, I'm wondering, would you, would you tell it about the night before Christmas?

Bill: Ooh, yes, I'd like to.

Noodles: You know that's my favorite story. "The Night Before Christmas." You won't forget to tell it now, will you?

Bill: Oh, no, no, I promise.

Noodles: Okay. Well, well, good-bye, good-bye. Oodely, oodely.

Bill: Good-bye, Noodles. Good-bye. We'll see you Christmas Day.

(MUSIC - THE END)

A Picture for Pondering

by Rasmussen

The Kind of Bath for Me

You can take a <u>tub</u> with a <u>rub</u> and a <u>scrub</u>

    in a two-foot tank of tin,

You can stand and <u>look</u> at the whirling <u>brook</u>

    and think about jumping in;

You can chatter and <u>shake</u> in the cold black <u>lake</u>,

    but the kind of bath for me,

Is to take a <u>dip</u> from the side of a <u>ship</u>,

    in the trough of the rolling sea.

Dear teacher, on some leisurely evening, sit down in your living room and read this poem aloud until it rings like an old familiar ballad. For a discussion of the use of rhyme scheme in word-unlocking see TE p. 45 at the back of this book.

Above all, keep the poem moving at a lively pace. It's a boy's poem, a seaman's poem, a man's poem, and, of course, that includes all the girls because sooner or later they identify with men. Think what a lovely choral reading and choral speaking experience for you and all of the children throughout the rest of your lives.

You may lie and <u>dream</u> in the bed of a <u>stream</u>

    when an August day is dawning,

^{it is}
^{it's} Or believe <u>'tis</u> nice to break the ice

    on your tub of a winter morning;

You may sit and <u>shiver</u> beside the <u>river</u>,

    but the kind of bath for me,

Is to take a <u>dip</u> from the side of a <u>ship</u>,

    in the trough of the rolling sea.

by Sir Edward Parry,
picture by Eric Carle

The Park

I'm glad that I
Live near a park

For in the winter
After dark

Here is a simple but quietly moving poem that children will take to their hearts with but a few readings. Thereafter, it will become a favorite choral speaking selection in your class.

The park lights shine
As bright and still

As dandelions
On a hill.

by James S. Tippett, picture by Gilbert Riswold

Stopping by Woods on a Snowy Evening

**by Robert Frost,
picture by Ed Young**

The wonder and the beauty of a poem like this should
never be distilled and mutilated by comprehension questions. It's quite enough for children to hear the poem
and ponder its meanings. Of all the people who respond
to this great poem by Robert Frost, children will most
clearly intake its meanings; for who have more promises
to keep—and intuitively know it—than children?

Whose woods these are I think I know.
His house is in the village though;
He will not see me stopping here
To watch his woods fill up with snow.

My little horse must think it queer
To stop without a farmhouse near
Between the woods and frozen lake
The darkest evening of the year.

He gives his harness bells a shake
To ask if there is some mistake.
The only other sound's the sweep
Of easy wind and downy flake.

The woods are lovely, dark, and deep.
But I have promises to keep,
And miles to go before I sleep,
And miles to go before I sleep.

Isn't it interesting that the last word of the third line in each stanza introduces the rhyme of the subsequent stanza? And isn't it predictable that the last stanza would bring the interlocking pattern to a peaceful halt?

Tomorrow

> when the wind is high
I'll build a kite to ride the sky,
Tomorrow, when the wind is high.

Tomorrow when the waters gleam
I'll build a boat to sail the stream,
Tomorrow, when the waters gleam.

Tomorrow when the roads run far
Across the hills, I'll build a car.
I'll build a car with shining wheels
To pass the other automobiles,
Tomorrow, when the roads run far.

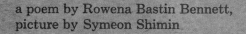

a poem by Rowena Bastin Bennett,
picture by Symeon Shimin

Even the title here suggests rollicking nonsense. To read deep psychological meanings into this doggerel denies the whimsical clues in the art and text. But if you are therapy oriented, don't forget that humor itself is one of man's best ways for encompassing and enduring the human situation.

Can the Matter be?

Something is the matter with Roger.
He thinks he is handsome.
There must be something the matter
with Roger to think he is
handsome.

Nothing is the matter with Harry
　　He knows he is not handsome.
To be sure he is unhandsome,
　　he breaths fire.

Oh dear! What!

story by Bill Martin Jr., pictures by Risa Glickman, lettering by Ray Barber

Everything is the
matter with Peter.
He knows everything
is the matter
so he acts like a
hippie.

Only one thing is
the matter
with Myrtle.
She is pretty.
She'd rather be
pretty than
be a dragon.
Her mother
can't change
her mind.

146

Not a thing is the
matter with
Joseph.
He looks like a
crocodile
but when you're
a dragon,
it doesn't matter
if you look
like a crocodile.

Look what is the matter
with Steven.
His tongue is stuck.
It is stuck outside.

Josephine also is stuck. She is stuck in her stocking. Being stuck in a stocking is a serious dragon matter.

Horace also has a serious matter. He has three heads. "But this is good," says Horace. "Three heads are better than one in working out a problem."

Sylvester is lucky.
He has found
a way
to solve his problem.

Mary is not lucky.
Her problem is
running away
with her.
Some problems
are like that.

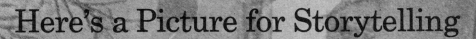

Here's a Picture for Storytelling

by George Buckett

What is happening in this picture, children?

This straightforward story calls for a straightforward reading. Its beauty is in the repetitive, cumulative action and in the ring of well-tempered language. The episodes of the story have been marked to cue the crescendos and rallentandos in reading. The climax of this story is surprisingly quiet—followed by a rather long, but deeply satisfying, epilogue that restates the entire story idyllically; *i.e.,* it restates the story action without the story problem.

The Big Cheese

by Miriam Schlein,
pictures by Joseph Low

Introduction
Once there was a farmer who made a big cheese.

It was yellow, and mellow, and round.

It was a most beautiful cheese.

"Without a doubt," said the farmer,

"this is the best cheese

that has ever been made in all the land."

"I think you are right," said his wife, taking a sniff.

"Take it to the market. It will fetch a good price."

"No," said the farmer.

"The best cheese in all the land—who should eat it? A forecast of the story problem.

Not just anybody! No," he said proudly.

"I am going to present this cheese to the king."

"The king!" said his wife. "To the king?"

"Of course," said the farmer.

"And even the king, when he has tasted,

will agree that this is the finest cheese

he has ever had in his life!"

He placed the big cheese carefully in a wheelbarrow.

His wife draped it over with a snowy white linen napkin.

And the farmer went down the road,

pushing the cheese before him.

Episode 1. He did not go too far, when he met a goatherd,
herding along a flock of goats.

"What are you pushing along in that barrow,
my friend?"
called out the goatherd.

"A cheese," replied the farmer,
setting down the wheelbarrow gently.
"I am on my way to present it to the king,
for it is the finest cheese
that has ever been made in the land."

"Indeed?" said the goatherd.
And is it made of goats' milk?"

"No," said the farmer. "Cows' milk."

"Then how," replied the goatherd,
"can it be the best cheese ever made?
The finest and richest and best cheeses
are always made from goats' milk."

"How?" said the farmer indignantly. "This is how!"
He flung the napkin off. And there sat the cheese—
that beautiful, yellow, mellow cheese.

"It does look fine," agreed the goatherd.
"But have you tasted it?"

"Of course not," said the farmer.
"You can see it is still whole."

"Then how do you *know*
it is the finest cheese ever made?

We must taste it, here and now,"
said the goatherd, pulling out a knife.

"Stop!" cried the farmer.

"How can I present the king with a cheese
that has a piece cut out of it?"

"But how can you
present the king with a cheese
you do not know tastes the best?"

The story problem. Isn't it interesting that at this point, we can begin to hunch that the cheese will be eaten before the farmer gets to the King!

"You are right," said the farmer. "Cut."

The goatherd cut out a large triangular slab.

This he cut in two,

half for the farmer, half for himself.

They each took a small taste.

"Indeed," sighed the goatherd.

"It is a fine-tasting cheese."

They sat in the shade, under a tree, nibbling cheese.

The goats nibbled the grass in a circle, all around them.

When they were finished, the farmer sprang up.

"I must be on my way," he said.

"I, too," said the goatherd. "Go well, my friend.

I must admit you have made the finest cheese

a man could make,

out of goats' milk, *or* cows' milk."

Episode 2. The farmer beamed.

He threw the napkin over the cheese and went on his way.

He followed the road over hill and dale.

As night began to fall, he came to an inn.

"I will stop here," he thought.

"I will have a bite to eat and get a good night's rest,

and early in the morning, I shall be on my way."

He pushed open the door,

which entered into a cheerful room,

all set with tables and cloths.

To one side, a big fire crackled in the fireplace.

Before the fire sat a fat, rather jolly-looking man.

Note that this and the next episode are a repetition of the action in Episode 1. This is a basic pattern found in many contemporary stories and folk tales. Children love the predictability of a story pattern like this.

Have you noticed that this entire story has been printed in units of meaning that ignore the traditional concept of paragraphing but that simplify the reading?

"Come in," cried the fat man.

"The innkeeper is in the kitchen, fixing my meal.

But come warm yourself by the fire, my friend.

I am a traveler like yourself."

The farmer parked the barrow with the cheese

carefully away from the heat of the fire.

"And what have you there,

that you treat with such care?"

asked the man, curiously.

"I treat it with care indeed," replied the farmer.

"For this is a cheese, which I am taking to the king."

"To the king?" said the traveler.

"But the king has the most skilled cheese-makers

right at the palace!"

"But my cheese is the best

that has ever been made in the land," said the farmer.

When each line of type in this story is analyzed for its basic *chunks of meaning*,
you can readily see the thought units that a good reader deals with sequentially,
either when he is reading silently or orally. As children learn to see and hear and
anticipate these patterns of meaning in language, their comprehension as well as
their rate of reading will tend to increase.

"The best?" repeated the traveler. "How do you know?"

"I know," said the farmer, proudly.

"Besides, the goatherd agreed with me."

"The goatherd!" said the traveler.

"The goatherd may know about goats—

but what does he know of the king's taste for cheese?"

"I tell you what," he went on. "Sit down. Relax.

Do me the honor of dining with me.

After we have wined and dined,

and our stomachs are contented,

then *we*," he said, pointing to himself,

"then *we* will taste your cheese.

For it does not do to taste cheese when one is very hungry.

For then almost anything will taste delicious.

No, the time to taste cheese for delicacy of flavor

is when the stomach is already contented.

That is the way to taste cheese.

Ask me, my friend. I know!"

"But I want to present my cheese to the king!"
cried the farmer.

"Of course," said the traveler. "Don't fear.

We will just take a teeny taste. It won't even be missed.

Come now," he beckoned. "Here is the dinner.

Sit down with me, and enjoy it."

The farmer sighed, and sat down.

Presently the innkeeper came
and set before them all sorts of steaming hot dishes.
One was a platter of roast duck,
all crispy and brown on the outside.
There was stuffing, and brown gravy with mushrooms.
There were buttery beans and carrots,
and a tray of fresh-baked bread.
And to drink, there was a pitcher
of foamy homemade root beer.

"Ah," sighed the farmer, when they were finished.
"That was a meal to remember."

"And now," said the jolly traveler
sitting up in his chair, so that his big round body
seemed to fill every inch of it.
"Now we come to the treat of the meal.
Now we taste the cheese."

"The cheese," said the farmer.
"Are you sure you want to taste it now?
Aren't you a bit full?"

"Of course I'm full, of course," cried the jolly traveler.
"But if your cheese is as truly delicious as you say—
we will enjoy it even if we are full as full as full.
Bring it on!"
He whisked the napkin off the cheese.
"It *looks* good," he said.
Then he cut the cheese and took a small wedge.

He bit into the soft center,
and crushed the cheese on his tongue,
and swallowed.

"But the taste," he cried, striking the table.
"The taste is magnificent!
I have never tasted as good a cheese—
not even one made by myself!"

He wiped his hands of the crumbs.

"I must take another small piece."

"Mmmm," said the fat traveler,
with his mouth full.
"Mmmm. My friend," he said. "You are right.
This is a cheese fit for the king.
I'll take just one more taste."

"This is the last," promised the jolly traveler,
carving a large slice. "But here," he said.
"Don't you want a piece for yourself?
You haven't had any at all!"

"Oh, I'm too full," said the farmer unhappily,
as he watched his big cheese get smaller and smaller.

"There," said the fat traveling man, wiping his lips.
"Take it away."

The farmer leaped up, threw the napkin over the cheese,
and trundled it away. Then he said goodnight
and went up to his room to sleep.

Episode 3. In the morning early, the farmer awoke
and had a hearty breakfast.

Then he took his wheelbarrow, with the cheese,
and trundled it down the road.

It was a lovely day, sunny and bright.

The road led straight along.

The farmer walked briskly,
past field upon field of tall golden corn,
with tassels bending in the breeze.

And soon, in the distance,
he saw tall spires,
reaching into the sky.
"The king's palace,"
he said.
"I am there at last."

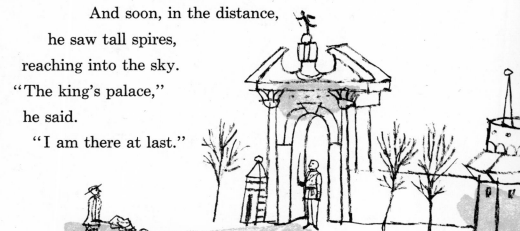

He straightened his shirt, pulled up his socks,
and presented himself at the palace gate.

"Who are you, and what do you carry?"
asked the guard at the gate.

"I am a farmer," said the farmer.
"And this is a cheese I have made for the king."

"That door," said the guard.
He pointed across the courtyard,
to where three young fellows were stringing beans,
and a woman was beating a batter.

"There is the royal kitchen."

"But this cheese is to be presented to the king himself!"
said the farmer, determinedly.

"Then that other door," said the guard.
He pointed to a high, arched doorway.

The farmer trundled across the courtyard
and through the high arched door.
He found himself alone in a large hall.

But from behind a closed doorway
at the other end of the hall, he heard a hum of voices.

Presently the door opened and a man came out.
He was dressed in elegant ribbons and silk,
with a plumed hat on his head.

When he saw the farmer and his barrow,
he said, surprised, "Eh, what is that?"

"A big cheese," said the farmer.
"I wish to present it to the king."

"A cheese, you say?" said the man with interest.
"Ah, a bit of cheese would taste good."

"Besides," he added, "I am the king's taster.
Whatever the king eats, I must taste first.
To make sure it is all right, you understand.
I had best do it now."

He bent down and with his silver penknife
cut off a wedge of the cheese.

"Indeed," he said, with his mouth full.
"It is a fine cheese."

"Now, may I present it to the king?" asked the farmer.

The taster's mouth was too full to answer.
Just then, the door opened again
and another man came out.
He was even more elegantly dressed than the first,
in varying shades of deep maroon,
with tassels and braids of gold.

"What are you doing?" he asked in amazement,
seeing the farmer with the barrow,
and the first man with his silver penknife in hand.

"Cheese," the first man managed to say. "Very good."

"Ah," said the second man,

unclasping a little gold penknife, and making a cut

Another, then another of the king's men came out.

Soon there were seven, all standing about,

with their delicate little knives in hand,

all munching on the cheese.

Episode 4. Presently still another man came out
from the room at the end of the hall,
closing the door behind him.

He was of medium height, the same as the farmer.
He had a ruddy face, as if he spent
much of his time out of doors.

And he was not dressed as splendidly
as the other men of the court.
but the other men stepped back
when he approached. "What is this?" he said.

"A cheese, sir," said the farmer, stepping forward.
"The best that has ever been made in all the land.
And who should eat the best cheese?
Not just anybody. No.
It is a cheese fit for a king.
And that is why I am here.
I have come to present it to the king!"

"Indeed?" said the ruddy-faced man, lifting the napkin.

The farmer stared. For what was left of his big cheese?
Not a half. Not even a quarter.
Just a small piece stood there, amidst the crumbles.

The ruddy-faced man bent down,
and reached for the last piece.

"Stop!" cried the farmer.

His voice rang out in the large hall.

"Stop, stop, STOP!"

The story is building to a climax strongly, but you'll observe that the climax itself is understated and, therefore, quiet and gentle.

The others looked up in amazement.

"Excuse me," said the farmer, sadly.
"But I meant this cheese for the king.
And you are taking the very last piece.
Well, take it," he said, turning sadly.

"It doesn't matter now.

I traveled all this way,

but I can't present the king with just a scrap.

Go on," he said. "Finish it."

★ "But I am the king," the ruddy-faced man said, softly.

"The king!" said the farmer. "A thousand pardons!"

He bent his head, and fell to one knee,

nearly tipping the barrow as he did so.

"Come," said the king. "Get up.

A thousand pardons? A thousand pardons for what?

For your loyalty to the king?

For wishing to present to him the finest cheese

you have ever made in your life?

★Here is the climax. The King has tasted the cheese. The problem is resolved after a fashion—not as the farmer hoped for, but it could have turned out worse.

"Come now," he said.

"There is nothing to pardon. Get up."

The farmer got up, all red in the face.

"May I have this last piece of cheese now?"
asked the king with a smile.

"I do love cheese, you know."

"Of course," the farmer nodded.

The king ate the piece of cheese.

"It is the finest cheese I have ever tasted
in all my life!" he said.

"And I thank you."

The farmer beamed. "But such a small piece was left,"
he said. "I am sorry."

This forecasts
the long epilogue
that follows. "Look here," said the king.

"This is not the last cheese
you will ever make in your life, is it?"

"No." The farmer shook his head.

"Well then," said the king,
"when you make another cheese
which you feel you would like me to have,
just bring it around.

And do not let anyone taste it first," he added.

"I will trust your very own judgment."

To this the farmer agreed.

Then he trundled his empty wheelbarrow back home,
whistling all the way.

The Epilogue.

How glad he was to be home!

He told his wife his adventures.

Then he busied himself on his farm

with his chickens, and his soft brown cows,

and his asparagus and pumpkin garden.

And of course, he made cheeses.

They were fine cheeses, yellow

and mellow and round.

But somehow, none seemed yellow

and mellow enough so as to be fit for a king.

Many months passed. Almost a year.

Then one day, the farmer ran in, to his wife.

"I have made one!" he cried. "At last!"

"Fit for a king?" asked his wife.

"Fit for a king!"

Observe how the epilogue satisfies the children's wish
for the farmer to succeed in his original purpose.

With not another word,

they placed the big cheese on the wheelbarrow.

The farmer's wife covered it

with a gleaming white linen napkin.

And the farmer set off, down the road,

to the palace of the king.

Not the goatherd,

nor the jolly traveler,

nor the king's own men,

nor anyone else took a taste of *this* cheese.

This cheese the farmer presented to the king

round, and complete, and unbroken.

It was every bit as good as the first one.

It was a cheese fit for a king!

That is what the king said.

And he should know!

excerpted from translations by George W. Cronyn, painting by B. L. Nichols

The highly formalized language of these Navajo Indian chants
soon will become compulsive rhythms like the beat of a tom-tom.
Children will need to hear them several times and to join in reading them aloud before they become familiar, but then the chanting
will well up like a great symphony. This, of course, is what the
Navajo himself experiences in the treasury of these chants. How
important this is—this passing on of the human tradition of chants.

Songs of the Navajo

In beauty may I walk.
All day long may I walk.
Through the returning seasons may I walk.
On the trail marked with pollen may I walk.
With grasshoppers about my feet may I walk.
With dew about my feet may I walk.
With beauty may I walk.
With beauty before me, may I walk.
With beauty behind me, may I walk.
With beauty above me, may I walk.
With beauty below me, may I walk.
With beauty all around me, may I walk.
In young age wandering on a trail of beauty,
    lively, may I walk.
In old age wandering on a trail of beauty,
    lively, may I walk.
It is begun in beauty.
It is begun in beauty.

painting by Maynard Dixon

In this age of concern for the environment, nothing is more significant than putting children in
touch with the Indian's deep reverence for
Mother Earth. The message here is especially
strong because the language and art embrace the
Indian tradition. At some time, you may find
these chants particularly effective for dramatiz-
ing the Indian culture. The children will enjoy
dancing the rhythms, pantomiming the meanings
and intoning the pleas. What a refreshing anti-
dote to the stereotype picture of "the Indian"
which children are often imprisoned with.

The curtain of darkness is hanging,
From the land of night it is hanging,
Before me, in beauty, it is hanging,
Behind me, in beauty, it is hanging,
Above me, in beauty, it is hanging,
Below me, in beauty, it is hanging.
How joyous the darkness!
Hanging before me,
    behind me,
        above me,
           below me,
How joyous, how joyous the stars!

The curtain of daybreak is hanging,
The daylight curtain is hanging,
From the land of day it is hanging,
Before me, as it dawns, it is hanging,
Behind me, as it dawns, it is hanging,
Above me, in daylight, it is hanging,
Below me, in daylight, it is hanging,
How joyous the daylight!
Hanging before me,
    behind me,
       above me,
          below me,
In beauty,
In beauty it is hanging!

painting (next page) by Cornelius Salisbury

Beauty before me,
With it I wander.
Beauty behind me,
With it I wander.
Beauty below me,
With it I wander.
Beauty above me,
With it I wander.
In young age traveling,
With it I wander.
In old age traveling,
With it I wander.
On the beautiful trail I am,
With it I wander.

painting by F. Koufmann

Thonah! Thonah!
There is a voice above
Sounding in the dark cloud,
The voice of the thunder
Thonah! Thonah!
Thonah! Thonah!
There is a voice below,
The voice of the grasshopper.
The earth is rumbling
From the beating of our basket drums.
The cloud is rumbling
From the beating of our basket drums.
Everywhere humming,
Everywhere rumbling,
Everywhere raining,
Raining,
Raining.

painting by Maynard Dixon

That flowing water!
That flowing water!
My mind wanders across it.
That broad water!
That flowing water!
My mind wanders across it.
That old age water!
That flowing water!
My mind wanders across it.

watercolor by Allen Reinhold, painting (next page) by Cornelius Salisbury

In beauty have I walked.
All day long have I walked.
All life long have I walked.
Through the returning seasons have I walked.
On the trail marked with pollen have I walked.
With grasshoppers about my feet have I walked.
With dew about my feet have I walked.
With beauty have I walked.
With beauty before me, have I walked.
With beauty behind me, have I walked.
With beauty above me, have I walked.
With beauty below me, have I walked.
With beauty all around me, have I walked.
In young age wandering on a trail of beauty,
      lively, have I walked.
In old age wandering on a trail of beauty,
      lively, have I walked.
In old age wandering on a trail of beauty,
      living again, may I walk.
It is finished in beauty.
It is finished in beauty.

drawing by an unknown artist

Here is an easy-moving little story that children can successfully read on their own. However, you will all probably enjoy yourselves much more if the story is read aloud. You will notice that it is written more like a play than a story, and it begs to be read in parts. We have marked the parts for you.

*COUNTING
LIGHTLY

by Leonard Simon,
pictures by Ted Schroeder

If you read this story as a play, leave out phrases like *Dim thought, he said*, etc.

                                                    for you   to the hilltop
Father: "Come on, Dim. It's time∧to go∧

Today you will learn to be a hunter."

Dim: "Today is the day," thought Dim.

"I will be a great hunter like my father.

I'm coming, Father! I'm ready!"

Father: "And what are you going to do with that spear, Dim?"

Dim: "I'm going to hunt buffalo."

Father: "Yes, but first you must learn to find them.

Do you see that tree?

Go hide under it.
                                                    quickly
If you see any buffalo, come back and∧tell me."

Throughout this book we have expanded simple sentences by adding describing words and/or phrases and clauses. We have used this mark ∧ to indicate the additions. For a discussion of expanding sentences see p. 80 of the essay at the back of this book.

Dim: "Whew! It's hot up here!" thought Dim.

"Hunting is hard work.

I haven't seen a buffalo all day.

Gee, I'm tired.

Maybe I can take a little nap."
will
should

A stage direction: _{looked}
_{sat}

Dim jumped up.

Dim: "What was that?

What makes the earth shake so?

I see them now.

There are the buffalo.

There are so many of them.

There are more than a dog has legs!

There are more than I have friends!

_{run and}
I must tell everybody!"
_{my father}

198

A stage direction:

Dim ran down the hill, _as fast as he could go_

Dim: "I found them!

I found the buffalo!" he shouted.

Father: "How many, Dim? How many did you see?"

Dim: "I saw more than a tree has branches, _How many would this be?_

more than there are stars in the sky."

Sister: "Oh Dim, you did not," said his sister.

"You're just making it up."

Dim: "I am not!" said Dim.

"I saw a whole bunch."

Sister: "How many?" _set group herd_

Dim: "I don't know."

Father: "Dim," said his father, "a great hunter must know

how many animals he sees."

Dim: "All right. I'll go back and look, _buffalo I see_

and then I'll tell you how many."

Dim: "But how can I count all the buffalo?" thought Dim.

"I wish I could carry each buffalo back.

That way I would not have to count them.

But they are too heavy.

I will never be able to be a hunter."

A stage direction:
Dim lay down on the hillside.

Dim: "Lying on the rocks hurts my knees.

The rocks! That gives me an idea!

I know how I can count the buffalo."

Announcer:
How do you think Dim will be able to count the buffalo?

200

Dim: "I cannot carry buffalo.

But I can carry rocks.

One rock for one buffalo.

Another rock for another buffalo.

This is easy. _{for anyone as smart as I am}

Now, all I have to do is carry the rocks

down the hill."

Do you think people
ever did use objects like
rocks for counting?

Here's a picture for picture reading.

Dim: "These rocks are ^(too) heavy," said Dim.

"I don't think I can carry them all.

It's hard to carry rocks

and slide down the hill at the same time.

Oops, dropped one.   Notice how totally reduced
—————————————   this sentence is.
Oops, there goes another!

I can't carry so many in my hands.

I saw more buffalo than I have rocks.

I dropped buffalos... I mean

A stage direction: I dropped rocks all the way down the hill."

Everybody laughed.

Father: "Dim, isn't there something lighter than rocks

that you could carry?"

Dim: Dim thought, "I always carry wood for the fire."

"I know," he said.

"I'll carry back a stick of wood for each buffalo.

There are many sticks up ^(there) on the hill."

Dim: "This is easy," said Dim. ^to himself

^simple
"One stick for one buffalo.

Two sticks for two buffalo.

Another stick for another buffalo."

A stage direction:
Soon Dim had a pile of sticks—

one stick for each buffalo.

Dim: "This pile of sticks is hard to carry. ^but if I am careful I can do it

There, I came all the way down the hill

and didn't drop one.

Now, everybody can count my sticks.

The number of sticks is the same

as the number of buffalo."

Sentences can be expanded by adding phrases
and clauses as well as single words.

204

Dim: "I saw as many buffalo as I have sticks," said Dim.

"Now you can see how many buffalo there are.

But my arms hurt from carrying the sticks.

I'm getting too tired to hunt.

I wish there were a lighter way to count."

Sister: "Dim," said his sister,

"you could count the buffalo with only one stick."

Dim: "I could not!" said Dim. "There are many buffalo."

Sister: "Come on," said his sister, "I'll show you.

Just bring that long stick and that rock."

Announcer: Can you guess how Dim's sister

will count the buffalo?

is counting
counted

Isn't it interesting that
you can also spell this word
buffaloes or *buffalos*?
How about:
potato   potatoes
tomato   tomatoes

Sister: "Now Dim, you watch, me carefully" said his sister.

"There is one buffalo.

I make one mark on the stick.

There is another buffalo.

I make another mark on the stick."

Dim: "Now I see, how you are doing it" said Dim. "I can do the rest."

A stage
direction: Dim brought his stick to his father.

Dim: "See how many buffalo there are!

And it isn't so hard to carry just one stick."

Sister: "Dim," said his sister, "you can count
without carrying anything."

Dim: "Count without carrying anything? How?"

Sister: "Use your fingers. Look, Dim!

represents
stands for
takes the place of

One finger for one buffalo.

Why can't we say "One finger is one buffalo?"

Two fingers for two buffalo.

Another finger for another buffalo."

Dim: "Is that so! But I don't *have* enough fingers

to tell how many buffalo I saw."

Sister: "It doesn't matter, Dim.

When you use up all your fingers,

you can start over again."

Dim: "That's silly."

stupid

Did you ever stop to think that you are born with a perfect set of counters—your fingers? Have you used these counters in your lifetime?

Sister: "When you use up all your fingers,

just think *all*. Since you have 10 fingers, *all* means ten.

Here, I'll draw a picture to show you.

See, these are like the marks on the stick.

This many means *all*.

So, you saw *all*-and-two buffalo."

10

A stage direction:
Dim looked at his sister.

she had drawn
He looked at the picture of the stick.

ALL

Dim: "You never use rocks, or sticks, or fingers.
How come you can count?"

Sister: "Oh, I use words," said his sister.
"I made up names to count with.
And using counting names is easy—
all you have to do is remember them.
You can think them, and say them,
and write them, and read them.
And they are never heavy to carry."

Dim: "And then," said Dim,
"you really are counting lightly."

POOR OLD LADY she swallowed a fly,
I don't know why she swallowed a fly.
Poor old lady, I think she'll die.

POOR OLD LADY she swallowed a spider.
It squirmed and wriggled and turned inside her.
She swallowed the spider to catch the fly.
I don't know why she swallowed a fly.
Poor old lady, I think she'll die.

POOR OLD LADY she swallowed a bird.
How absurd! She swallowed a bird.
She swallowed the bird to catch the spider,
She swallowed the spider to catch the fly,
I don't know why she swallowed a fly.
Poor old lady, I think she'll die.

POOR OLD LADY she swallowed a cat.
Think of that! She swallowed a cat.
She swallowed the cat to catch the bird.
She swallowed the bird to catch the spider,
She swallowed the spider to catch the fly,
I don't know why she swallowed a fly.
Poor old lady, I think she'll die.

POOR LADY she swallowed a dog.

> She went the whole hog
>
> when she swallowed the dog.

She swallowed the dog to catch the cat,

She swallowed the cat to catch the bird,

She swallowed the bird to catch the spider,

She swallowed the spider to catch the fly.

I don't know why she swallowed a fly.

Poor old lady, I think she'll die.

POOR LADY she swallowed a cow.

> I don't know how
>
> she swallowed the cow.

She swallowed the cow to catch the dog,

She swallowed the dog to catch the cat,

She swallowed the cat to catch the bird,

She swallowed the bird to catch the spider,

She swallowed the spider to catch the fly,

I don't know why she swallowed a fly.

Poor old lady, I think she'll die.

POOR LADY she swallowed a horse. She died, of course.

an old jingle

Here's a choral reading that will brighten many a day, with a cumulative structure that is only broken at the end. For a discussion see TE p. 32.

Here is a sensitively told story about a child's wondering. *Why do living things kill one another?* This is Paulossie's question. Children do wonder about things like this and they need to read stories that help them understand. Invite the children to follow in their books while you read aloud. Certain children may also wish to join in the reading. Let them. You will both profit.

★ # Paulossie

Pronounced
Paw-low-see

AN ESKIMO BOY

story and photographs of Eskimo stone carvings created by Robert C. Swim

This is a totally bare sentence. It cannot be reduced.

This is Paulossie.

He lives in the North,

Northern Canada

where the wind blows strong and cold.

But Paulossie is not cold.

He wears the sealskin parka

and the sealskin boots called *komiks*

that his mother made for him.

Pronounced Tah-goo'-nah

Paulossie's father, Tagoona, is a good hunter.

He has a pair of good binoculars

and a powerful rifle.

One day Paulossie borrowed his father's binoculars

and went up to the high rocky hill behind his igloo.

He wanted to watch the animals that lived on the ice.

Through the binoculars Paulossie watched

two walruses sleeping on the ice.

We have suggested ways for reducing many of the sentences in this story. It is important for the children to read the sentences in their original and reduced forms. This helps them recognize that there is such a thing as sentence style and that recognition of sentence style (in this case reduced or expanded) helps with word unlocking.

~~Suddenly~~ he saw a great polar bear

swimming toward the two sleeping walruses.

The polar bear swam closer.

Then he ~~climbed onto the ice and with his teeth~~

grabbed the nearest walrus ~~by the nose and mouth~~

~~so that the walrus could not use its sharp tusks.~~

Children, let's try reading this sentence without the words *cried out and*. What do you think about the sentence when it has been reduced this way?

The walrus ~~cried out, and~~ fought the polar bear. But he was caught.

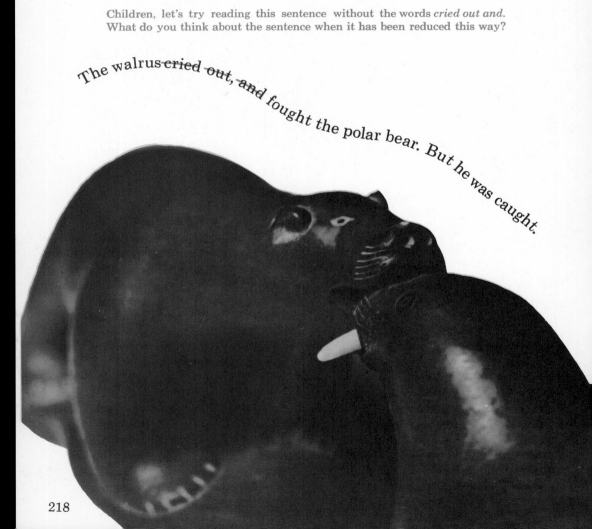

The other walrus woke up and slipped quickly into the water. There was nothing he could do to help his friend. It was too late. The polar bear was going to have his dinner. "Oh, The poor walrus," thought Paulossie.

Does this brief expansion help the sentence?

Presently,

∧Paulossie picked up the binoculars
and looked down on the lake at the foot of the hill.
He saw a little duck, swimming alone.
Suddenly a snowy white owl swooped down from the sky.
The duck dived under the water, but too late.
The owl caught the duck by the back of the neck
and lifted him out of the water.
Oh,
∧"The poor duck," thought Paulossie.
Paulossie stood up and started down the hill.
He felt very sorry about the walrus and about the duck.

We are beginning to sense Paulossie's problem.

Then,

^At the bottom of the hill Paulossie saw Niki,
one of his father's dogs.
Niki was chewing on a piece of ice-covered fish.
frozen
Tagoona, Paulossie's father,
had caught the fish through a hole in the ice,
and it had frozen solid as soon as it was taken from the water.
The fish Niki ate were always frozen.
He had to work hard for every bite.
each
Paulossie said, "Hello, Niki."

How do people show that they
But as Paulossie came closer, Niki growled. don't want anyone near them?
Niki did not like to have anyone near him when he was eating.
He was afraid his food
would be taken away from him.

"It is a very hard world," Paulossie said.

[1] "First I saw the polar bear attack the walrus. [2] Then I saw the snowy white owl attack the little duck. [3] And now here is Niki, growling because he is afraid I will take the fish."

Do all Eskimos live in igloos?

When Paulossie arrived home,
his mother Mary, was sitting in front of the igloo.
She was working very hard.
She was chewing a piece of <u>sealskin</u> to make it soft.

compound word

She was getting this piece of sealskin ready
to make komiks for Paulossie's little brother, Davidie.
If Mary didn't chew the sealskin,
it would be too tough to make into komiks.
It would cut the threads
when she sewed it,
and the water
would seep through
and wet little
Davidie's
feet.

So Mary had to make the sealskin soft before she sewed it.

Mary looked up as Paulossie came near the igloo.
looks down   comes

"You look sad, Paulossie," she said.

"What is the matter?"

"I think it is a very hard world, Mother,"

said Paulossie.

[1] "This morning I saw a polar bear attack a walrus

that was sleeping on the ice.

Paulossie is putting his problem into words. Is there any solution to this kind of a problem?

[2] I saw a snowy white owl swoop down on a little duck.

[3] Then Niki growled at me when I came near him

while he was eating a fish.

Why is it that way?"

Mary slowly pushed back the hood of her parka.

Quietly she began,

"Do you remember when you were a baby,

how you cried when we had no food to give you?"

"No," said Paulossie.

"I was too little to remember."

Mary said,

"Do you remember when you were a small boy,

and your father could not catch any animals or fish?

Do you remember how you cried

from the pains in your stomach?"

"Yes," said Paulossie, "I remember that." What is the first thing you remember? Do you remember ever being uncomfortable or crying because you were hungry?

"Within all creatures," said Mary,

"there is a voice that cries, 'Live! Live! Live!'

When we do not listen to that voice,

it makes us hear it in another way.

All creatures have pain when they are hungry,

or when they are very tired, Mary is giving Paulossie an explanation that will help him solve his problem.

or when they are cold."

You've probably noticed in our annotations the lack of "comprehension" questions that demand "right" answers. This we have done deliberately. We have formulated open-ended questions which make any child's response relevant, knowing that in the cross-firing of opinions, children will arrive at valid comprehension of the points at issue. When children sense that all responses are respected, they feel free to let you know who they are, both as individuals and as children learning to read. Thus, children who are responding to open-ended questioning do arrive at precise meanings when precise meanings are appropriate, but they achieve these meanings through the cross-polination of varied points of view rather than through the stilted right-wrong edict of textbooks or teacher. The ability to amalgamate many points of view into an answer or working solution is basic to problem solving in a democratic society. We should be developing this kind of skill at every opportunity.

"If we do not have enough to eat,
When
our stomachs pinch and hurt us.

If we do not get enough sleep,

our eyes and our head hurt.

If we do not dress warmly enough,

we shiver

and shake,

and our teeth

begin

to chatter."

Parka

Here's a picture for
picture reading.

The Eskimo carvings pictured here
are not large. Most of them are
not more than 6 or 8 inches high.

Komiks

"Many times you have seen
your father standing
beside a hole in the ice,"
Mary said,
"out in the cold
for hours and hours.
He is waiting
for a seal
to come up for air.
When it does,
your father is able
to harpoon the seal,
pull it out of the water,
and quickly butcher it
right there on the ice
before it freezes solid.
If he waited,
he would not be able
to cut the seal
with his knife.
Then he sews up the seal

Why does he
sew the seal? and brings it home
on a sled.
That is how we get
sealskins to make clothing,
and oil for our fire,
and food
for our hungry stomachs.
If your father
did not harpoon the seal,
we would not stay alive."

"When we are young, our parents

  help us to stay alive.

When we grow older,

  we must take care of ourselves.

One day soon, Paulossie,

  you will go with your father

to harpoon the whale and the walrus,

  for you, too, must learn how

to keep yourself alive.

That is also why

  he traps the fox,

and goes out in his kayak

  to harpoon the whale and the walrus.

We must have the skins

  and the oil and the meat to live.

[1] All creatures want to live,"
   living things

Mary continued.
   said, added

"The polar bear attacks the walrus

  because he wants to live.

[2] The owl attacks the little duck

[3] and hungry Niki guards his food

  because they want to live.

[4] And your father stands out in the cold,

  near a hole in the ice,

waiting to harpoon a seal,

  because he wants to live."
          survive

Here's a picture for picture reading.

Kayak

Just then Little Davidie
came out of the igloo.
He came out to see
if his komiks were finished.
But he was not dressed
for the cold air.

warmly
properly
adequately

"Paulossie," said Mary,
"will you take Davidie
would you mind taking
back inside the igloo, please,
until I finish his boots?
He is in a hurry for them."
"Yes, I will, Mother,"
said Paulossie.
Paulossie took Davidie
inside the igloo.
Mary finished
softening the sealskin
for little Davidie's komiks.
Paulossie played
with his little brother
while they waited for Tagoona
to come home
with something to eat.
Already
Paulossie's stomach
was telling him
it was time for supper.
suppertime
time to eat

Do you think Paulossie's problem
was really solved?

The Snare

I hear a sudden cry of pain!

    There is a rabbit in a snare:

Now I hear the cry again,

    But I cannot tell from where.

But I cannot tell from where

    He is calling out for aid;

Crying on the frightened air,

    Making everything afraid,

Making everything afraid,

    Wrinkling up his little face,

As he cries again for aid;

    —And I cannot find the place!

And I cannot find the place

    Where his paw is in the snare;

Little one! Oh, little one!

    I am searching everywhere!

by James Stephens,
picture by Cynthia Koehler

tasty
wretched
disgusting
miserable
pesky

try as I might
since I wasn't there
so I can't tell
for the life of me

I   don't know   why she swallowed a

surely
certainly
really

When children add describing words to expand simple sentences, they learn much about how words fall into place in English sentences. Not only can they enjoy their new sentences, but they can analyze the effect the addition of describing words has on sentences. As children recognize where various kinds of words, as describing words, fall in English sentences, they have a highly useful word-unlocking skill—one that is developed throughout the SOUNDS OF LANGUAGE program.

PUZZLE

and saved her life.
and lived happily ever after.
and become famous.
to let in some air.
that flies are not for eating.

fly.

when she could have swallowed ice cream
when she could have chewed tobacco
when she could have played the piano
when she only opened her mouth
when her mother always told her

THIS ANNOTATION IS MEANT FOR THE NEXT PAGE. WE HAD A SPACE PROBLEM AS YOU CAN SEE ⟶

A child who can figure out where this song starts and follow it to completion is telling you a lot about his intuitive linguistic abilities. Offer no help. Let the children solve the riddle.

How much longer can you make this sentence by adding single words and clusters of words?

WHEN SAMMY PUT THE PAPER ON THE WALL HE PUT THE PARLOR PAPER IN THE HALL. HE PAPERED ALL THE CHAIRS HE PAPERED UP THE STAIRS HE EVEN PUT A BORDER ON GRANDMA'S SHAWL.

236

WHEN SAMMY PUT THE PAPER ON THE WALL.

STUCK TOGETHER

WHEN SAMMY

W

UPON US ALL.

A FEATHER WE ALL

LIKE BIRDS OF

HE SPILLED THE POT OF THE PASTE

a traditional song,
drawing and lettering
by Bob Shein

WHEN SAMMY PUT THE PAPER ON THE WALL

Verse 1　When I was just a little girl (boy)

　　　　I asked my mother, "What will I be?

　　　　Will I be pretty (handsome)? Will I be rich?"

　　　　Here's what she said to me:

　　Chorus　"Que sera, sera,

　　　　Whatever will be will be;

　　　　The future's not ours to see.

　　　　Que sera, sera!

　　　　What will be will be!"

Whatever Will Be, Will Be

Verse 2　When I was just a child in school,

　　　　I asked my teacher, "What should I try?

　　　　Should I paint pictures? Should I sing songs?"

　　　　This was her wise reply:

Verse 3　When I grew up and fell in love,

　　　　I asked my lover (sweetheart) "What lies ahead?

　　　　Will we have rainbows day after day?"

　　　　Here's what my lover (sweetheart) said:

Verse 4　When I have children of my own,

　　　　They ask their mother (father) "What will I be?

　　　　Will I be pretty (handsome)? Will I be rich?"

　　　　I tell them tenderly:

a song by Jay Livingston and Ray Evans   picture by Zunia

Tiger Boy

An original fairy tale by
Paulette Washington, age 10
pictures by Ed Fowles

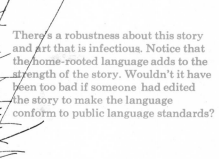

Way in the country
in a little house
lived a boy named Bill
but people called him
Tiger Boy
because he liked tigers.
Every morning
he would go looking
for a tiger
but instead of finding
    a tiger
he found a cat
and named it Tom.
It was a gray and white
    cat.

Every morning he would feed the cat
except for one day
when he didn't have any food.
So Tom got angry
and began to bite Tiger Boy
and Tiger Boy got angry too,

and picked up Tom
and put him in a cage
and kept him in there.

Then he heard a knock at the door.
It was a big old lady
and before Tom asked her her name,
he said, Have a seat.

Then he said,
My name is Bill,
and the old lady said,
My name is Mrs. Clark.
I was looking for a home
until I came to this house.
Is this your cat?

Yes,
said Tiger Boy,
his name is Tom.
I put him in the cage
because he was
hungry
and I didn't have
any food to give him.

Oh! said the old lady. I have plenty food and plenty money

Many stories including this one are a person's dreams of wish fulfillments. Children like writing this kind of story.

for you and me.

Half the time they munched the grass,

and all the time they lay

Down in the water-meadows,

the lazy month of May,

A-chewing,

A-mooing,

To pass the hours away.

The rhythm for reading this with a musical lilt has been scored with a long mark to indicate both a heavier accent and a slightly longer beat than you will give the dot. The effect is a skipping, light-hearted chant.

Voice 1:
"Nice weather," said the brown cow.

Voice 2: "Ah," said the white.

Voice 1:
"Grass is very tasty."

Voice 2: "Grass is all right."

Read as a conversation. Ignore the rhythm.

All: Rhythmically again.

Half the time they munched the grass,

and all the time they lay

Down in the water-meadows,

the lazy month of May,

A-chewing,

A-mooing,

To pass the hours away.

1. "Rain coming," said the brown cow.

2. "Ah," said the white.

1. "Flies is very tiresome."

2. "Flies bite."

250

Half the time they munched the grass,

and all the time they lay

Down in the water-meadows,

the lazy month of May,

A-chewing,

A-mooing,

To pass the hours away.   1. "Time to go," said the brown cow.

2. "Ah," said the white.

1. "Nice chat." 2. "Very pleasant."

1. "Night." 2. "Night."

All: Very softly and slightly slower.

Half the time they munched the grass,

and all the time they lay

Down in the water-meadows,

the lazy month of May,

A-chewing,

A-mooing,

To pass the hours away.

by James Reeves, picture by Mamoru Funai

After children get the sounds and the swing of this delightful cow-talk poem, they will have continuous fun doing it as a choral reading. And all the while, they will be familiarizing themselves with the sounds and structures of language—and at the same time perfecting their reading skills.

O, what a romantic bit of fluff to deposit in your linguistic storehouse! If you can get a recording to play, the children will sing — and read — this in five minutes flat. (Hopefully not too flat!)

I'm looking over a four leaf clover that I overlooked before;

One leaf is sunshine, the second is rain,

Third is the roses that grow in the lane,

No need explaining the one remaining is somebody I adore

I'm looking over a four leaf clover that I overlooked before.

a song by Mort Dixon, illustration by Lynda Barber, handlettered by Ray Barber

The Story of TOM THUMB

Traditional, adapted by Bill Martin, Jr.
Pictures by Peter Lippman

Introduction

Once on a cold winter night long, long ago,

Once upon a time

a woodcutter sat by the fire,

stirring the flames with a stick.

His wife sat near him,

at her spinning wheel, working.

"Oh, I wish we had a child," he said.

"All I hear is the sound of the wind

whistling at the door.

I would much rather hear

the sound of children playing on the floor."

"Yah, yah," said his wife. "If only we had a child,

even if he were no bigger than my thumb,

that would be having my heart's desire."

fondest wish
best dream

255

Some stories are hung together around a problem. Recognizing the problem helps unravel the story. Here is the problem in which this story is rooted. See TE p. 43.

In due time, a child was born

to the woodcutter and his wife,

and though he was perfect in every way,

alas! he was no bigger than his mother's thumb.

He was so small that his mother could cradle him

in the palm of her hand.

"Oh, what a beautiful child he is,"

said the woodcutter's wife.

"Yah, yah," said the woodcutter.

"He's the handsomest child in the village."

CLOSE BEFORE
STRIKING

Though they fed him plenty of rich nourishment,

Although

he grew no larger and remained always

the size that he was first born,

no larger than his mother's thumb.

And they called him *Tom Thumb*.

One day many years later, when Tom's father
was going into the forest to cut wood,
he chanced to say, "Oh, if only I had someone
who could bring the horse and the cart
to me this afternoon,
it would make my work so much easier."

"I can bring the horse and cart to you, Father,"
said Tom.

"How could you do that, Tom?
  You are so little,
  you could not hold the reins in your hands."

"I don't need to hold the reins, Father.
  If Mother will harness the horse to the cart
  and put me in the horse's ear,
  I'll simply tell the horse which way to go."

"Do you think it will work, Tom?
  Very well, we'll try!"

So late that afternoon,
Tom's mother hitched the horse to the cart
and put Tom Thumb in the horse's ear.

Tom waved goodbye.

Then he shouted, "Gee up! Gee up!"

and the horse started down the road,

quite as if someone were sitting on the driver's seat,

~~tugging at the reins and telling him which way to go~~.

Can you tell when reducing a sentence changes the meaning and when it does not?

As the horse was turning a corner

and going into the woods

and Tom was shouting, "Gee up! Gee up!"

two strangers passed by.

The first stranger said, "This is very odd.

I see the horse, I hear the driver.

But alas! I cannot see him!"

"This is very odd, indeed!"
said the second stranger.
"Let's follow that horse and cart
and see to whom they belong."

Here is a forecast of a problem that will be the basis for a good story.

The two strangers followed along until the horse
reached the spot where the woodcutter worked.
Tom Thumb called out, "Whoa! Here I am, Father,
with the horse and cart, just as I said.
Come take me from the horse's ear."

The woodcutter lifted the little boy
from the horse's ear
and held him in the palm of his hand.

The two strangers were surprised to see Tom Thumb.
They had never seen a child so small.

The first stranger said, "Let's buy that little boy
and show him on the street corners in town.
We'll make a fortune."

The second stranger said, "Didn't you hear?
He's a woodcutter's son.
The woodcutter will not sell his own son."

Many stories such as this one are a series of related episodes, each part distinctive
but dependent on the other parts for wholeness. The episodes in "Tom Thumb" are
identified to enhance your enjoyment of this particular story form and also to cue
you in reading the story aloud. There is a natural rising and falling of intensity
within each episode. The end of each episode is a psychological breathing place, as it
were, before engaging in the next adventure.

"Then let's take him," said the first stranger.
"There are two of us, but only one of him."

So the first stranger approached the woodcutter
and said, "Sell us that little boy, woodcutter.
We'll see that no harm comes to him."

"Oh, no, no!" said the woodcutter.
"I wouldn't sell my own son."

But Tom Thumb had overheard the evil men talking
and quickly climbed up to his father's shoulder
and whispered in his ear,
"You might as well take their gold, Father,
because they plan to carry me off, anyway.
But don't worry! I'll be home soon, very soon!"

Now we have a serious problem. The story will concern
itself with the resolution of this problem.

And so it was that Tom Thumb was sold
for a double handful of gold,
and the tiny boy was carried away
by the two strangers.
He sat on the brim of the taller man's hat
and watched the countryside
as the strangers walked along the road.

At eventide, the two men were tired
from having walked so long and so far,
and they sat down at the crossroads to rest.
Tom Thumb was tired, too,
from having sat so long,
and he begged to be put down upon the road
to stretch his legs.

This was when the two strangers
made their mistake!
For when Tom Thumb was put down upon the road,
he darted off into a cornfield
where he found a mousehole just his size.
And he slipped down into it.

Just before he disappeared from sight,
he called out, "Goodbye, you evil men!
Your gold has fallen into a mousehole!
You'll never find me!"

The two men were angry.
They ran up and down the rows of corn,
punching sticks into every mousehole,
but alas! they could not find Tom Thumb.

At last it became dark
and the two men had to hurry on their way,
because they knew their wives
were waiting supper on them.

When Tom Thumb was certain
that the two strangers had left,
he crawled out of the mousehole.
He didn't want to chance meeting
a big ferocious animal, like a mouse,
in its hole after dark.
So he walked along a row of corn
until he found a snail shell just his size.
He curled up in it and fell asleep.

But no sooner was Tom Thumb asleep,
when he was awakened by two robbers talking.

The first robber said,
"Let's go to the rich man's house
and steal his gold and silver."

The second robber said,
"How can we get into his house?
There are heavy iron bars at the window."

Tom Thumb called out, "I can help you!"

"Who said that?" asked the first robber.

"I did," said Tom Thumb.

"I am right at the toe of your boot.
  Don't move your foot,
  you might step on me.
  Just follow the sound of my voice
  and you'll find me."

  The first robber grabbed Tom Thumb
  and held him tight in his fist.
"You little imp! How can you help us?"

"Oh, I can help you," said Tom.
"You want someone to walk through
  the iron bars of the rich man's house
  and hand out his gold and silver?
  I am the very person who can do that."

  The robber smiled.
"Young man, you have quite a wit about you.
  We can use you!"

The robbers sneaked to the rich man's house
and put Tom Thumb on the window sill.
He was so small that he simply walked between
the iron bars and made his way into the house.

As soon as he was out of reach
of the robber's long arms,
he called out loudly,

"Shhhhhh!" whispered the robbers.
"Do you want to awaken everyone in the house,
   you little fool?"

What do you want first, the gold or the silver?

The housemaid awakened.
She lit a candle and came down the stairs,
looking fearfully about.
"What's going on down here?" she asked.

On hearing someone coming,
the robbers turned and fled into the forest.
They were never heard from again.

The housemaid looked all about,
behind the doors and under the chairs,
but she found no one.
Tom Thumb was hidden behind an envelope
on the rich man's desk.

Convinced at last that she had only been dreaming,
the housemaid blew out her candle and went back to bed.

Tom Thumb waited until the house was quiet.
Then he slipped down from the desk
and out through the window.
He made his way to the barn,
where he found a nice warm spot in the hay
and fell asleep.

When it was morning,

a milkmaid came to the barn

to feed and milk the cow.

The first bundle of hay

that she tossed into the cow's manger

was the bundle in which Tom Thumb was sleeping.

When Tom awakened,

he found himself in a cow's mouth,

about to be chomped by the teeth!

He tried to escape
but the cow's tongue pulled him back,
and Tom Thumb found himself on a long slide,
slipping down to the cow's stomach.
When he reached the bottom,
he looked around and said,
"My, it's dark down here.
When they made this place,
they forgot to put in a window."

In the meantime, the cow was eating hay,
and the hay was coming down the slide
into the stomach.
It was too crowded for poor Tom.
He called out,

"No more HAY, please! There's enough down here!"

Now, the milkmaid was seated on her milking stool,
milking the cow.
When she heard the cow speaking,
she became so excited that she fell off her stool
and spilled the bucket of milk.

The milkmaid ran to the house crying,
"Master! Master, come quickly!
The cow's gone crazy!
The cow is talking!"

"Not the cow, but you have lost your sense,"
said the rich man.
However, he followed the milkmaid
to the barn to see what was happening.
As they came through the door,
the cow was still saying,

No more **HAY**, please!
There's enough down here!

The rich man now thought the cow
was possessed by evil spirits,
and he ordered the cow killed.

The cow was slaughtered

and her stomach was thrown out on a dunghill.

Episode 5.

Tom was just freeing himself from the stomach,

when out of the woods there came

a great, gray, hungry wolf.

With one gulp, he swallowed Tom Thumb!

Poor Tom! He was becoming discouraged.

Trouble seemed to follow him wherever he went!

Oh, Mr. Wolf! Are you hungry?

Yes, wolves and boys are always hungry.
What about girls?

"Then I can tell you where you can find
some tasty food," said Tom.
"Just follow the path through the woods
to the woodcutter's cottage.
Crawl through the drainpipe into the storeroom,
and there you'll find ham and cheese
and pickled eggs and smearcase
cottage cheese
and spiced beets and boiled pigs' feet.
All of the good food that you could possibly want!"

The wolf didn't wait to be told twice
where to find a meal,
for his hunger was great.
He ran down the path through the woods
with his tail flying behind him
and Tom Thumb riding in his stomach.

When the wolf came to the woodcutter's cottage,

he did just as Tom had told him.

He crawled through the drainpipe to the storeroom

where he found all of the good food

that Tom had described.

The wolf ate and ate and ate . . .

and ate . . . and . . . ate.

At last he had his fill.

Notice how the punctuation predicates the emphasis in reading this sentence.

He turned back to the drainpipe to escape,

but alas! he had grown so fat

that he could not get out.

This was exactly what Tom Thumb had <u>counted on!</u>

Episode 6.

Tom called out, "Father! Father! Come save me!

I'm home! I'm home! I'm home!"

Now Tom's voice didn't sound as loud

as you might think, because, remember,

Tom was inside of that wolf.

His voice sounded more like this:

Father! Father! Come save me!
I'm home! I'm home!
I'm home!

Notice how the eye guides the ear in the reading of this speech.

Here is the climax of the story.

Fortunately, Tom's father was a light sleeper.

He heard Tom calling and he jumped out of bed.

His wife was right behind him.

They ran to the storeroom and opened the door.

When they saw the wolf,
the woodcutter grabbed an axe
and his wife grabbed a butcher knife.
Then they took after the wolf.

Oh, Father! Please be careful with that axe!
I'm inside of this thing!

Tom's father was careful, indeed.
With one well-placed blow of the axe,
he killed the wolf and Tom was rescued.

The story actually is over at this point, but many stories, this included, have a slightly prolonged closing that gives the reader a chance to live a little longer within the spell of the story and to drink in the emotional and mental impact of the story meanings.

The woodcutter held Tom in the palm of his hand, and said, "Welcome home, Tom! Welcome home, son!"

Tom's mother was so happy that she began to cry. "Tom, Tom," she cried, "where have you been?"

"Mother, I've been in a mousehole,
  I've been in a snail's shell,
  I've been in a cow's stomach,
and I've been inside of a wolf.
But from now on I'm going to be happy
just to stay home and sleep."

And that is exactly what Tom Thumb did.
He curled up in his mother's thimble
and he slept all of that morning
and half of that afternoon—
which is a long time for any boy to sleep.

Go back now just to look at Peter Lippman's illustrations
for the story. What satire! What tongue-in-cheek humor!

Four Little Foxes

Speak gently, Spring, and make no sudden sound;
For in my windy valley, yesterday I found
New-born foxes squirming on the ground—
    Speak gently.

Walk softly, March, forbear the bitter blow;
Her feet within a trap, her blood upon the snow,
The four little foxes saw their mother go—
    Walk softly.

Go lightly, Spring, oh, give them no alarm;
When I covered them with boughs to shelter them
    from harm,
The thin blue foxes suckled at my arm—
    Go lightly.

Step softly, March, with your rampant hurricane;
Nuzzling one another, and whimpering with pain,
The new little foxes are shivering in the rain—
    Step softly.

by **Lew Sarett**

"Four Little Foxes" is an experience—nay an adventure—in humanness. Its value is in
direct proportion to its contribution to the reader's emerging humanity. Thus, the reader's
willingness to be sensitive to the human dimensions of a poem or story or drama, even
though the main characters are objects or creatures other than human, may be counted as
a reading skill. One needs systematic experiences in giving himself over to intense feelings
and longings like these. If the children want to react verbally to the poem, welcome their
comments, but don't press for such a discussion. Feelings are a reaction in and of themselves.

Teacher's Edition

Part One

The Heart of the Program

The *Sounds of Language* reading program
is a fresh and enchanting collection
of poems, stories, articles, and pictures
that realistically prompt children to hear the spoken patterns
of the sentences they read.
As children gain skill in using their ears
to guide their eyes in reading,
they have a qualitatively different reading experience.

Consider the young child
who has frequently heard his teacher read
"*Ten Little Indians.*
Once a child has these sounds
clearly and solidly in his ear,
he has little difficulty reading this old rhyme
in its printed form.
Once his ears begin telling him
what his eyes are seeing,
he approaches the reading with confidence and expectation.
And when he comes to his teacher and exultingly declares,

I know that word, Miss Barber!
That word is "little!"

she has evidence
that he is relating sight and sound in reading.
And it is easy for her to take this child a step further
by asking him if he can find the number 4,
or if he can find the word *Indian.*
It should not surprise you to know
that even at the first-grade level,
a child is already something of an expert
in analyzing language,
a fact overlooked in most reading programs.

ttle Indians, 4 little, 3 little, 2 little Indians, 1 little Indian boy. 1 little, 2 little, 3 little Indians, 4 little, 5 little, 6 little

Think of the three-year-old child on a bus
who says,

> *I rang the bell.*

a sentence sound he learned by listening.
At age four, he is apt to say,

> *I ringed the bell.*

a sentence sound that he never in his life heard.
Why then does he say it?
A child at four no longer simply imitates language sounds
that he hears in his environment.
He is beginning to figure out how language works
and how to make it work for him.
When he says, *I ringed the bell,*
he gives evidence that he is analyzing language
and that he knows how to change a verb
from present to past tense.

In similar ways in the *Sounds of Language* program,
a child is helped to become more and more expert in
using and analyzing language.
The aim is to help him become aware
of what he intuitively knows about language,
and to help him explore and verbalize
old and new learnings.

10 little, 9 little, 8 little Indians, 7 little, 6 little,

10 little Indian boys.

7 little, 8 little, 9 little Indians, 10 little Indians,

—from *Sounds I Remember*

Language analysis emerges in abundance
at all levels in *Sounds of Language*
because the program is a total language and esthetic experience
which logically and comfortably connects a child
with his past experiences in using oral language
and with his intuitive knowledge of how language works.

Too many children in school have come to know reading
as word calling and drill,
with little or no opportunity
to claim language in its many dimensions.
The purposes of this teacher's edition, therefore,
are to help you join children and support them

1) in their growing appreciation of literature and language;

2) in a useful inquiry into how language works,
both in its oral and written traditions;

3) in a useful inquiry into literary structure; and

4) in the development of esthetic awareness.

The pages of the pupil book (incorporated in this teacher's edition)
have been annotated for your convenience.
The annotations appear at the precise spot on the page
where they are needed to point up learning insights
and teaching strategies.

At no time is an annotation so prescriptive
that it precludes your insights from the teaching process.
To the contrary, the annotations are geared
to triggering all your insights and hunches
in helping children *latch on* to language and their humanity.

There is nothing complicated about this method of teaching.
Once you have read this informal dialogue
and the annotated pages,
you will feel comfortably at home with the program.
In fact, you may find yourself thinking:
Here, at last, is a program that helps me
use all of my knowledge and intuitions about language
—and about teaching.

Now, let's talk informally
about ways for using the *Sounds of Language* readers
to bring new dimensions
into your teaching of reading.
We have no choice but to help
all children learn to read.
They inherit the need to read
simply by living in our culture.
We, therefore, have the obligation to provide
wide-ranging ways for unlocking print.

What works for one child
doesn't necessarily work for another child.
What works for one kind of reading material
doesn't necessarily work for another.
Children are highly inventive and insightful
in ways of unlocking print—
until unimaginative reading instruction
tells them there is only one way to decode,
"Sound out the words!"
Actually, there are dozens of ways
to unlock the printed page.
And there are dozens of ways
that lead into the act of learning to read
before successfully pulling together
ear and eye and tongue and muscle
in the mature act of reading.

Some boys we have known
seemed at first to read more with their feet
than they did with their eyes.
You've had these kinds of boys
in your own classrooms.

Aren't they interesting
as they screw themselves up
into impossible positions
and keep perfect time to whatever is being read?
We should be saying to these boys:

> *Henry, you're so great at reading*
> *with your feet! How would you*
> *like to try reading with your eyes?*

And Henry wouldn't mind at all—
in fact he might be delighted to try—
knowing his comfortable way for responding to print
has been so respected.
But unfortunately,
we don't recognize Henry's rhythmical body response
as a reading behavior,
accustomed as we are to thinking about reading
as an eye exercise
and a "sounding-out" ritual.
Instead of praising Henry
and helping him include other parts of his body
in his response to the printed page,
we are likely to admonish:

> *Now, Henry, sit up straight*
> *and pay attention to your book.*

If Henry had the skill of self-analysis
and dared challenge the teacher's edict,
he might respond:

> *But I am paying attention.*
> *Rhythmical body response*
> *is part of reading a book.*

Only Henry doesn't have the language
for verbalizing his intuitive response to print.
And unless we have the awareness
to recognize what he is doing,
another potentially successful reader
will start the long and uncomfortable journey
of finding out that there is something wrong
with his way for learning to read;
and another potentially fine teacher
will be thrown into miscommunication with a child
simply because the definition of reading behavior
which has been made available to her
through teachers guides and college courses
is too narrow to accept and encourage
the many-faceted reading behaviors of real live children.

The *Sounds of Language* program makes it easy and enjoyable
for children and teachers to explore and perfect
multiple ways for unlocking print
and enjoying the miracle of language.
Children will learn to figure out the pattern
back of an author's way of putting a story
or poem or sentence together,
and to use this information for reading words
they didn't know they knew.
They will learn to figure out the different shapes of sentences
and to recognize unknown words
largely by where they fall in a sentence.
They will learn to figure out rhyme schemes and read new words
by recognizing where they fall in a certain rhyming slot.
They will learn to figure out underlying rhythmical patterns
and to use syllabic patterns
as one way to take hold of unknown words.

All of this, at first, may sound strange and complex
if you have not observed children using these natural ways
for making a go of reading.
But this essay will help you discover a multiplicity of ways
for using literature to bring new dimensions
into the teaching of reading.
The program is based on only a few practical teaching strategies.
These strategies work in kindergarten
as well as they work in eighth grade and all up and down the line.
The children themselves modify the strategies
by their individualized responses.

Once you own these strategies,
you can forget about the teacher's guide
and look forward to relaxed and creative reading sessions
where you are free to respond
to the children's individualized responses
and where you have a structural know-how
to help them learn to read.

The teaching strategies
explored in this essay are: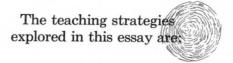

1) Recognizing That Language Works in Chunks of Meaning

2) Reading Aloud to Deposit Literary and Linguistic Structures
in Children's Storehouses

3) Innovating on Literary Structure to Claim Basic Patterns

4) Figuring Out How Stories and Poems Work

5) Helping Children Verbalize Their Intuitive Literary Insights

6) Figuring Out How Sentences Work

7) Innovating on Sentence Patterns

8) Figuring Out How Words Work

9) Figuring Out How Print Works

10) Developing Skill in Comprehension

11) Linking Writing to Reading

12) Cultivating Literary and Esthetic Appreciation

13) Developing Sensitivity to the Three Levels of Language

14) Developing Sensitivity to Humanness

—drawings from "My Mother is the Most Beautiful Woman in the World,"
Sounds of a Young Hunter

Learning to read
is not something that happens
after a stereotyped readiness period
in first grade or kindergarten.
Learning to read
is the job of a lifetime.
Two-and-three-year-old children who are read to a lot
begin their reading careers early.
The day a child gets hold of a sentence pattern that works for him
and reads it into the telephone directory
or the Montgomery Ward catalog
or his daddy's newspaper at night,
he is launching himself on his reading career.
He is role-playing himself as a successful reader.
The day a child reads a book from memory,
he is furthering his reading career.

He, in truth, is finding joy and power
in the pages of a book,
a psychological posture that every successful reader
continuously brings to each reading encounter,
knowing, subconsciously if not consciously,
that he can make a go of print.
This is the first and foremost reading skill.

Part Two

The Teaching Strategies for Sounds of Language

Whether it be at home or at school,
when children are read to,
they begin their naturalistic ways
for latching on to print
and they continue to expand and refine these ways
throughout the course of a lifetime—
provided they are given helpful opportunities.
The *Sounds of Language* teaching strategies
will help you provide these opportunities
for children to respond to print
in naturalistic intuitive ways;
and they also will help you release children
to verbalizing their intuitive responses to language and print,
and develop them into word-unlocking skills.

1 RECOGNIZING THAT LANGUAGE WORKS IN CHUNKS OF MEANING

As each of us learned to speak the language,
simply by imitating the speech sounds that we heard,
we learned to cluster words into meaningful units within a sentence.
Even as babies using nonsense syllables,
we used intonation and clustering
to create a *sound of sense*.
Later as we learned vocabulary and sentence ways,
we made full use of sentence sounds (sometimes called melodies)
demonstrating that we intuitively understood
that language works in chunks of meaning.
Not once did we isolate the word sounds
from the sentence sound in which they were cast.
Not one of us said,

> "*I* (pause) *want* (pause) *my* (pause) *mommy!*".

Rather "*Iwanmymommy!*"
came out as a meaningful linguistic whole,
a fluid sentence sound with a cultural melody
that conveyed both feeling and thought.
Unfortunately, language instruction in schools
has ignored the natural workings of language
by such unnatural techniques as

A) focusing word recognition skills on individual words
   rather than on the clustering of words within a sentence,

B) insisting on paragraph forms
   with rigid right-left hand margins that ignore
   the natural grouping of words within a sentence,

C) talking about word meaning as if a word
   actually has a meaning outside the context of the
   sentence in which it derived its meaning; and,

D) insisting that children in all of their school language activities
   perpetuate these misconceptions.

The poets, more than anyone else in our society,
have tended to improve
the communication potential of their writing
by arranging their words into natural linguistic clusterings.

All of us are familiar with the ragged right hand margin of a poem
and may never have stopped to think
why the sentences are written this way.
Just observe how Margaret Wise Brown
accommodates the lines in "Four Fur Feet"
to the chunks of meaning within each sentence:

OH, he walked along the river

on his four fur feet,

his four fur feet,

his four fur feet.

He walked along the river

on his four fur feet

and heard the boats go toot—O.

—*Sounds of a Powwow*

How different this is from a page of prose in an ordinary book
where each line must move rigidly
from a left hand margin to a right hand margin
with only the paragraph breaks
to give a feeling of structure to the printed language.
This inflexible technique cruelly severs words in half
in order to accommodate the margins,
as well as ignoring the natural clustering of words
into chunks of meaning within each sentence.
Let's see what a prose sentence would look like
if it were separated into its chunks of meaning
to enhance the linguistic design of the sentence
rather than the arbitrary width of the page.

> *Sometimes the male lions*
>
> *may help ambush the game,*
>
> *but more often*
>
> *they take their rest*
>
> *under shady trees*
>
> *and watch*
>
> *while the lionesses stalk*
>
> *and kill the game*
>
> *that will become a feast*
>
> *for all of the lions.*

—"King of Beasts," *Sounds of Mystery*

As you observed, this is a complex sentence to read
but how much easier it becomes
when it is printed in its chunks of meaning.
Each of these groups of words has a meaning
that is more important than any single word within the group.
The words in each group, therefore, must be read together
as a subset of the more important set, the sentence.
Each subset leads into the next,
gradually amalgamating into the whole meaning of the sentence.
One of the miracles of our language
is its way of working in chunks of meaning.

An experienced reader does not move through a sentence
by reading each word separately.
Even though language is not ordinarily printed in chunks of meaning,
he learns to see—and sense—the groups of words
that best create meaning.
When a sentence is written from margin to margin across a column or
a page, with no special emphasis on the chunks of meaning, the reader
must do the work of seeing the words in clusters that release meaning.

This, at first, is not an easy task, but it is rewarding
because, soon, the reader finds himself
able to manage material that ordinarily would have stopped him.
Consider the problem of an inexperienced reader
who breaks a sentence into malfunctioning units, like this:

1) *"Where has*

2) *Sallie been*

3) *asked*

4) *to keep*

5) *Halloween?"*

6) *asked they.*

—from "Tomson's Halloween," *Sounds of a Young Hunter*

Such a child has a comprehension problem immediately
because he has violated the linguistic units within the sentence.
Just try reading the sentence orally as it is grouped here
and you will shudder at the absence of the sound of sense.
*The only criterion for knowing a chunk of meaning when you see it
is to hear it.*
A child's intuition about language,
once he has developed the concept of chunks of meaning,
will lead him through the sentence this way,
simply because this is the way he would speak it
and thereby exploit its sound of sense:

1) *"Where has Sallie been asked*

2) *to keep Halloween?"*

3) *asked they.*

Recognizing That Language Works in Chunks of Meaning TE 15

Reading instruction that emphasizes single word recognition
above all else
actually creates reading problems for children
because units of meaning are torn rudely apart
and children are not freed
to use their accumulated linguistic insights.
The concept of chunks of meaning within a sentence
is not foreign to children,
because they naturally speak in chunks of meaning
as they frame their oral sentences.
They need only to be helped to see that they can recreate
these same chunks on the printed page,
even if books are not printed in this way.
Hopefully the day will come when books,
at least for elementary school children,
will have considerable material printed in spoken language patterns.

2 READING ALOUD TO DEPOSIT LITERARY AND LINGUISTIC STRUCTURES IN CHILDREN'S STOREHOUSES

Each of us has a linguistic storehouse
into which we deposit patterns
for stories and poems and sentences and words.
These patterns enter through the ear
and remain available throughout the course of a lifetime
for reading and writing and speaking.
The good reader is a person who looks at a page of print
and begins triggering patterns
that have been stored in his linguistic treasury.
These patterns range all the way
from the plot structure an author has used in a story
to the rhyme scheme that hangs a poem together,
to the placement of an adjective in front of a noun
as part of the shape of a sentence,
to the underlying rhythmical structure in a line of prose or poetry,
to the *ed* ending as part of the shape of a word.

As these various kinds of structures
are brought into play
as a result of encountering a new version
of the same old basic structure,
a child is able to figure out much of the new vocabulary
because he recognizes the similarity
between the new structure
and structures he has already claimed.
A poor reader is the person who looks at a page of print
and no patterns are triggered to help him unlock the page.
This can be because he has not been read or talked to very much
and therefore has not deposited
story and poem and sentence and word patterns
in his linguistic storehouse.
Or this lack of triggering can occur
even if he has been talked to a lot
if the oral language patterns are not the kind
he is encountering in print.
A Spanish-speaking child, for example,
has stored sentence patterns
where the adjective follows the noun.
This does not help him unlock English sentences
where the adjective precedes the noun.
He will first have to hear and store in his being
the typical shape of English sentences
before his linguistic storehouse can help him unlock English print.

Now you can see why reading aloud
the poems and stories in the *Sounds of Language* readers
is a continuing part of this reading program
for children of all ages throughout their school years.
Sometimes you are reading aloud and the children are listening,
sometimes you are reading aloud and the children are chiming in,
sometimes the children are reading in chorus,
sometimes the boys and girls are reading aloud in dialogue,
sometimes the children are chorusing a poem or story by memory,
sometimes you and the children are reading aloud together,
with the children following the print in their books
so their eyes can be seeing what their ears are hearing
what their tongues are saying.

Dust of Snow

The   way a crow
Shook down on me
The dust of snow
From a hemlock tree

Has given my heart
A change of mood
And saved some part
Of a day I had rued.

—"Dust of Snow" by Robert Frost, from *Sounds of a Young Hunter*

For example, a child who has heard frequently
and later read and chorused aloud "Dust of Snow,"
will have deposited within his linguistic treasury
a feeling for the sound and meaning of the word *rued*
that enhances his potential use of the word
in all kinds of communication—
reading, writing, speaking and listening.
He also will have a reservoir of potential
for shaping a sentence with the expertise
of this sentence shaped by a poet.
There is no better way for children to learn
to appreciate and use our language
than having broad and continuous experiences
that attune both the ear and the tongue—then later the eye—
to the rhythms, melodies and sounds of language.

Hopefully this reading aloud and language consolidation
will be accompanied by spontaneous body movement—
either the kind of swaying and clapping and shuffling
that children initiate on their own
or interesting movements suggested by you.
Whenever children engage their entire bodies
in their responses to print,
they have the best possible chance
to bring wholeness to the reading act
and intaking linguistic know-how.

3 INNOVATING ON LITERARY STRUCTURE TO CLAIM BASIC PATTERNS

One choice in deciding how to follow-up
your reading aloud of a story or poem
is to invite the children to utilize the author's pattern
for expressing their own thoughts.
By borrowing the underlying structure
of a poem or story or sentence that they have come to know,
they are involved in two linguistically sound learnings
as they hang their own ideas on that structure:

1) they are having intuitive experiences
   with the fact that stories and poems
   do have underlying structures,

2) they are building a bridge between
   the linguistic facts of their worlds
   and the linguistic facts of the printed page.

The invitation to "Write about anything you want to"
may fall heavily on the ears of a child
who doesn't own the basic language structures
to give wings to what he wants to say.

On the other hand, a child of seemingly meager vocabulary
can latch onto a structure that comes in through his ears
and deposits itself indelibly in his mind,
and suddenly find his vocabulary taking on new strength.

Christmas 1969

And lo it came to be
that she bore an infant
in the subway. Because
the apartment cost was
too high. She wrapped
him in paper towels
from a gas station. And
lay him on the cold walk-
way. The train rattled
by but no sound came
from him.

And it came to be
that friends heard of him
and came to see him.
They brought with them
gifts of grape drink, cigar-
ettes, and a few dollars.

—Kevin Clark, grade 6, Issaquah Valley School, Issaquah, Washington.

The *Sounds of Language* readers
make it possible for children of either rich or meager vocabulary
to find challenge in their new creations which come about
as they innovate on the dependable structures found in these books.
Your reading table may come alive
with fifteen new books (written by children)
each time you read a story or poem
and invite the children to borrow the structure
and to adorn it with their own thoughts and language.
What a wonderful source of material the reading table becomes
for the children's independent reading.
Since all of the innovative books
are built on structures which the children have already claimed
in read-aloud times with the *Sounds of Language* books,
the children will not only be able to read the new books more easily,
but they will be recognizing how useful

a person's knowledge about underlying structure
can be in helping him read.
Thus, children who have just finished reading:

Good night, Mr. Beetle,
Good night, Mr. Fly,
Good night, Mrs. Ladybug,
The moon's in the sky.

Good night, Miss Kitten,
Good night, Mr. Pup,
I'll see you in the morning
When the sun comes up.

—*Sounds of Home*

will tend to feel that they are meeting
an old friend when they come upon a child's innovated story:

Merry Christmas, Mr. Beetle,
Merry Christmas, Mr. Fly,
Merry Christmas, Mrs. Lady Bug,
Santa's in the sky.

Merry Christmas, Miss Kitten,
Merry Christmas, Mr. Pup,
I'll see you Christmas morning
When I open presents up.

Once the children have latched on to this notion
of borrowing a favorite literary structure for their own creations,
you will have many surprises in store.
Suddenly all of children's linguistic storehouse treasures
become available to them—
structures they have claimed both in and out of school—
and they begin to appear in the children's writing.
Imagine the surprise and delight of a fifth-grade teacher
who had asked his children to do a piece of writing
that would cause him to see pictures,
when a boy who had been considered an academic dropout
came up with this piece of writing:

The Frog

The frog in the pond a lony *(lonely)*
little fellow who lives with
the pussy wilow and the muss *(moss)*
who sits on a lilly like a bud wathing *(watching)*
the ixcitment of the day
when he sees a giant much bigger
than his size. He sits riady
coilled like a spring with bright
marrbled eys ready to dive
in the water and hid *(hide)* only to
disapear like mggic *(magic)* disgased *(disguised)*
with the polution of a once
lively and active pond.

—from Mr. Bredahl's sixth grade,
Roosevelt School, Minot, North Dakota

Where did the writing come from?
It has the ring of a poet,
yet the child obviously didn't copy it from print
for a poet would have grouped the words
into spoken speech units which this writing partially lacks.
Is this something this child heard
and deposited whole in his linguistic storehouse
and is now utilizing?
Or is it a combination of his own phrasing
and literary language he has stored?
The miracle is how beautifully and accurately
this boy has called upon his language storehouse
to fulfill his class assignment.
Luckily, this teacher did not feel
that it was *cheating* or *copying* or *uncreative*
to borrow literary lines and/or structure.
This is how a newcomer creates a language of depth and beauty.
Gradually he will transform and in other ways reshape
the language he has borrowed.
Meanwhile, in his borrowing,
he is role-playing himself as a distinguished user of language
and is tuning his ears to the beauty of speech.

Bruce's teacher experienced all of the wonder and surprise
of a genuine literary encounter
when she discovered these lines he had written:

Mystery of Bill Martin
True blue surprise rubbed over man's flat eyes
Truthful innocence scattered down Skinny's rectangular nose
—from Tucson Public Schools, class and grade unknown

Obviously Bruce has a well-stocked linguistic storehouse
and in self-selected ways he is experimenting
with combinations of words that please him,
albeit the sentence meanings are obtuse.

4 FIGURING OUT HOW STORIES AND POEMS WORK

Children like to figure out how things work.
From their earliest days
they are endlessly poking and pushing and pulling-apart
to find out what makes things go.
This is how they learned to talk.
They listened to the talk on all sides of them
and they began experimenting and figuring out how talk works.
Once they began to figure out what they needed to know,
they made talk work for them.

In a similar way,
when you read a highly structured story to children,
they will chime in with you long before you have finished the story:

Brown bear, brown bear,

what do you see?

I see a redbird

looking at me.

Redbird, redbird,

what do you see?

I see a yellow duck

looking at me. [1]

As you turn the page and the children burst out reading

Yellow duck, yellow duck,

what do you see?

knowing, without even looking at the print, how the story is working,
they are giving evidence
that they have not simply memorized the story.
They have figured out how the author put his story together
and they are using this information
to help them read pages you haven't even read to them yet.
Much of this kind of figuring-out is intuitive.
It goes on while you are reading aloud
and while the children are chiming the story along with you.
Your job is to help the children verbalize these intuitive insights
and to organize them into word-unlocking skills.
Knowing how stories and poems are put together
will therefore be a help both to you and the children.
To begin with, stories are a series of episodes
or happenings arranged in some kind of recognizable shape.
For our purposes we view an episode
as either an action within a series of actions
or a language pattern within a series of related language patterns.
In so far as possible, in designing the early *Sounds of Language* readers,
we have used the turning of the page to indicate a new episode.

[1] This story by Bill Martin appears
both in the *Kin/der Owls* and in the Level 1 *Instant Readers.*

In some stories, the episodes repeat one another.
We have called that kind of story structure *repetitive sequence*.

My name is Tommy.
I am not very big.

I am not as big as a goat.   EPISODE 1
A goat is bigger than I am.

I am not as big as a horse.   EPISODE 2
A horse is bigger than I am.

I am not as big as an elephant. EPISODE 3
An elephant is bigger than I am.

I am not as big as a whale.   EPISODE 4
A whale is bigger than I am.

I am not as big as a dinosaur.
                               EPISODE 5
A dinosaur is the
biggest thing I know.

—from "What Is Big?" *Sounds of Numbers*

Even on first acquaintance, a child will predict

1) that the pattern of phrasing will maintain,

2) that all of the creatures will be described as big/bigger,

3) that in each comparison, the last part of the first sentence becomes the first part of the second sentence.

When the children come to the last episode, numbered 5,
and the repetitive pattern breaks,
we have dramatically enlarged the new language pattern
to signal to the children that something has changed
and the repetition has stopped.
The enlarged type also is a semantic clue
that tends to trigger children
into use of the superlative form of the adjective *big*,
which in its own way
also signals the end of the comparative sequence.
These kinds of exaggerated clues help children learn to trust print,
knowing that an author will keep leaving visual clues
that help the reader decode.
Imagine a child's surprise, therefore,
to discover that the dinosaur is not *bigger than I am*
but is *the biggest thing I know.*
Couched as this variation is within so many dependable repetitions,
it does not cause a child to lose faith in structural repetitions,
but rather it invites him to develop another literary insight—
that when a repetitive pattern gets going,
the author will at some time break the pattern
in order to bring the story to an end.
His curiosity is, therefore, piqued
to predict ways the author can break a repetitive pattern.

Let's look at another example:

Round is a pancake,   EPISODE 1
Round is a plum,   EPISODE 2
Round is a doughnut,   EPISODE 3
Round is a drum.   EPISODE 4

Round is a puppy   EPISODE 5
　　　Curled up on a rug.
Round are the spots   EPISODE 6
　　　On a wee ladybug.

Here is the
pattern break
signalling
that the   Look all around,   EPISODE 7
story is   On the ground, in the air,
ending.   You will find round things
             Everywhere.

—from *Sounds of Home*

Although episodes 5 and 6 are patterned extensions
of the previous episodes,
the reliability of their beginning phrases
cues the children to predict
that they can make a go
of a somewhat different sentence.
And, when the children come to the last episode, number 7,
and it does not begin with the repeated phrase *Round is*,
they have a reliable clue for predicting
that this repetitive story is coming to an end.

And here's a repetitive pattern
that's worn smooth with a lifetime of continuations:

As wet as a [fish] — as dry as a bone;

As live as a bird — as dead as a stone;

As plump as a partridge — as poor as a rat;

As strong as a [horse] — as weak as a [cat] ;

As hard as a flint — as soft as a mole;

As white as a lily — as black as a coal;

As plain as a staff — as rough as a [bear] ;

As tight as a [drum] — as free as the air;

As heavy as lead — as light as a [feather] ;

As steady as time — as uncertain as weather;

As hot as an oven — as cold as a [frog] ;

As gay as a lark — as sick as a [dog] ;

As savage as tigers — as mild as a dove;

As stiff as a poker — as limp as a [hand] ;

As blind as a bat — as deaf as a post;

As cool as a [cucumber] — as warm as toast;

As blunt as a [hammer] — as sharp as an awl;

As flat as a flounder — as round as a [ball] ;

As brittle as glass — as tough as gristle;

As neat as a pin — as clean as a [whistle] ;

As red as a [rose] — as square as a box;

As bold as a thief — as sly as a [fox] .

—from *Sounds of Mystery*

Figuring Out How Stories and Poems Work TE 29

While most stories have more than one kind of pattern
in their make-up,
many of the *Sounds of Language* selections
have enough obvious repetitions in their underlying structures
that children are propelled into anticipating the next line or episode.
Naturally this is not an infallible method
of decoding print,
but it is highly useful in combination with
the many other decoding skills
which are developed in the *Sounds of Language* program.
Moreover, it releases children to a continuous flow of reading
without the traditional vocabulary breakdowns
that are engendered by word-by-word reading
and which rob the language of its melodies and structural rhythms.
Children enjoy the *aha!* feeling which comes
when they predict that the second and third billy goats[2]
will behave much the same as the first billy goat
and when they predict that much of the language (and action)
in the first episode will be repeated.
They feel that they have a successful hold on the story
in "The Three Little Pigs and the Ogre"[3]

when the first little pig outwits the ogre
and they predict that the other two pigs
will try to do the same.
When children make identification with a strong character,
such as Ol' Stormalong,[4] they will predict
that even when he turns into a cowboy and a farmer,
much of his talk and actions
will repeat the talk and actions of Ol' Stormalong, the sailor.
Once you are aware
that a repetitive sequence is one way
of arranging the happenings in a story,
you probably will think of many other stories
which are arranged in this style.
You probably will also remember
how easily the children were able
to take hold of those stories
when you read them aloud.
At the time, you may not have realized
that the children were not simply memorizing—
that they were responding to the reliable repetition
in the story structure.

"Blo-o-ows!
Thar she blows!"

S w o o s h!

"Hooray, a storm!" shouted Stormalong to the farmers.
"Now I can get the kinks out of my muscles.
Avast there, mateys! Storm ahead! All hands on deck!"

"Just sit down and rest yourselves,
me hearties," said Stormalong.
"I'll round 'em up,
just to get the kinks out of my muscles."

[2] "The Three Billy Goats Gruff," *Sounds of Laughter*

[3] *Sounds of Mystery*

[4] "How Ol' Stormalong Captured Mocha Dick," *Sounds of a Distant Drum*

Figuring Out How Stories and Poems Work TE 31

B) Cumulative Sequence

This is the house
   that Jack built.
This is the malt,
That lay in the house
   that Jack built.
This is the RAT
That ate the malt,
That lay in the house
   that Jack built.

—from *Sounds Around the Clock*

How pleasantly this old cumulative rhyme
falls into place.
Each new line (episode) adds a new thought
before repeating everything that went before.
Children who sense the cumulative nature of this story
have a lot going for them.
They know, for example, that all of each subsequent page
will be familiar to them
except for the one added thought.
They also know that each new page will have more type
than the preceding page
and that they will be able to easily read
this accumulating language because it is familiar.
Children, on the other hand,
who are taught to read word by word,
are often turned away from pages with a lot of type
because they do not have structural insights
to help them unravel the print.

Throughout *Sounds of Language* children will encounter
stories and poems and songs and jingles
put together with a cumulative structure.
Each new encounter will remind them
that their insight into new selections
is influenced by the fact
that the basic pattern of cumulative writing
has already been deposited in their linguistic storehouses
and is now available for a lifetime of use
in reading and writing and literary appreciation.

Just for fun, let's see at which point you sense
that "I Came to this Land"
is cumulative in structure.

> *When I first came to this land,*
> *I was not a wealthy man,*
> *Then I built myself a shack.*
> *I did what I could.*
> *I called my shack, Break-my-back.*
> *Still the land was sweet and good,*
> *I did what I could.*
>
> *When I first came to this land,*
> *I was not a wealthy man,*
> *Then I bought myself a cow.*
> *I did what I could.*
> *I called my cow, No-milk-now,*
> *I called my shack, Break-my-back.*
> *Still the land was sweet and good.*
> *I did what I could.*

—from "I Came to this Land," *Sounds Freedomring*

Up until the line in the second verse,
"*I called my shack, Break-my-back,*"
this structure obviously is repetitive,
but the use of this particular line in sequence with the new episode
is evidence for predicting
that this is both a repetitive and cumulative sequence,
and that each new episode will include
an accumulation of the man's previously named possessions.

Figuring Out How Stories and Poems Work TE 33

Thus, you can figure out all six verses of this story song
with just the following information:

> *I bought myself a horse,*
> *I called my horse, Lame-of-course.*
>
> *I bought myself a duck,*
> *I called my duck, Out-of-luck.*

Aha! Now you're sensing that each creature's given name
is rhyming with the categorical name of the creature—
another structural clue.
Now you have three kinds of literary structure
going for you—repetitive, cumulative and rhyme-rhythm.

> *I got myself a wife,*
> *I called my wife, Joy-of-life.*
>
> *I got myself a son,*
> *I told my son, "My work's done."*

Aha! The author now has broken the language repetition,
signalling that he has probably reached the conclusion of his story.
Observe the additional semantic shift
in the first word of the last chorus:

> ***For** the land was sweet and good,*
> *I did what I could.*

This indeed confirms the fact that the story is over.
Did you enjoy getting hold of the story
partly by recognizing how the author put it together?
That same *aha!* feeling of awareness
that came to you as you figured out the pattern
and then made the pattern help you read the story successfully
is the same feeling that children get
when they sense an author's plan.
At the end of this section on various types of literary structure,
you'll find suggestions
for helping children verbalize the *aha!* feeling
and developing it into a word-unlocking skill.

C) Interlocking Sequence

Sometimes the episodes in a story or poem or song
do not simply repeat or accumulate,
rather they interlock in an intriguing way.

The funny old man and the funny old woman
sat by the fire one night.
"Funny old man," the old woman said,
"I don't know what to do.
When I went to the barn to milk the cow,
the funny old cow wouldn't moo."

The funny old man scratched his head,
"I know what to do," he said.
"Take her to town to see Dr. Brown
and bring her home in the morning.
That's what you do when the cow won't moo."

"But she's out in the woodshed lying down.
How will you take the cow to town
and bring her home in the morning?"

"If she can't walk," said the funny old man,
"I'll push her in the wheelbarrow if I can
and bring her home in the morning."

"But the goat's asleep in the wheelbarrow.
Where shall I put the goat?"

"Put the goat on top of the garden gate.
The goat can sleep there very late
till the cow comes home in the morning."

"But the rooster is roosting on the garden gate.
Where shall I put the rooster?"

"Put the rooster in the butter churn,
so tight that he can't twist or turn
till the cow comes home in the morning."

"But . . ."

—from "The Funny Old Man and the Funny Old Woman,"
Sounds of Laughter

Are you caught up in the intrigue
of this sequence, and ready to predict the

"But..." (says the old woman)

"Put..." (says the old man)

pattern on which this story is built?

Even if you had never learned
to sound out the word *butter*,
you are prepared to read this word in this story slot

"But my nice fresh butter is in the churn.

Where shall I put my butter?"

knowing how it interlocks with the preceding lines

"Put the rooster in the butter churn

so tight that he can't twist or turn

till the cow comes home in the morning."

Finally in this humorous story
when the old man says,

"Put the pig on a pillow in the feather bed,"

and the old woman says,

"No,"

instead of

"But,"

you know for sure that the interlocking pattern has been broken
and the story is coming to an end.

Now to exploit your structural know-how,
have a go at this:

I came to the river...

and I couldn't get across,

I jumped on a frog 'cause I thought it was a hoss,

The hoss wouldn't pull so I traded for a bull,

The bull wouldn't holler so I sold him for a dollar,

The dollar wouldn't pass so I threw it in the grass,

The grass wouldn't grow so I traded for a hoe,

The hoe wouldn't dig so I traded for a pig,

_ — — squeal _ _ — _ _ wheel,

_ — — run _ _ — _ _ gun,

_ — — shoot _ _ — _ _ boot,

_ — — fit _ _ thought I'd quit

And I did.

—an old rhyme, Sounds of Mystery

Think how much vocabulary is unlocked
simply by recognizing that these lines
interlock with one another
rather than simply follow one another.
You probably remember adult stories
where some happening triggered off
or brought together a chain of events,
such as in *The Bridge at San Luis Rey*
or Chaucer's *Canterbury Tales*.
Even the reading or viewing of Shakespearean plays
is both simplified and intensified
when you recognize the interlocking relationships
of characters.
The moment you con Lady Macbeth
or Claudius or Petruccio, for example,
you begin predicting events and language.
What a reading skill!

D) Familiar Cultural Sequences

Simply by living in our culture,
children have certain built-in structures going for them
that can be put to work in learning to read.
They know, for example, that the hours of the day,
the days of the week, the months and seasons,
the number system and the alphabet
have dependable sequences.
Sooner or later
children become familiar with and use these sequences
like another hand or foot or ear or eye
in dealing with the outside world.
The *Sounds of Language* program
exploits certain of these structures
as another way to help children appreciate the fact
that the recognition of underlying sequence
is an aid in decoding print:

In the first month of the year
I found one brown pony
and he followed me home.

In the second month of the year
I found two white kittens
and they followed me home.

—from "One, Two, Three, Four," *Sounds of Numbers*

Children are now prepared to read the words *third* and *three*
because they sense that along with the repetition
in this story
is a reliance on ordinal and cardinal numbers.
Similarly,

On Monday I make strong boxes . . .

On Tuesday

I make

narrow boxes . . .

—from "A Maker of Boxes," *Sounds of Laughter*

children who have never seen the word *Wednesday*
anticipate that it will be used in the next episode,
and will read the word in its appropriate slot,
confirming the fact that they recognize
the author's basic way of organizing his story.
It's a proud triumph for a reader.

Seventh graders can enjoy unlocking print
by using a familiar cultural sequence (the alphabet)
that has been with them since nursery school days:

A you're adorable, **B**

you're so beautiful, **C** you're a

cutie full o' charms **D** you're a

darling, and **E** you're exciting.

and **F** you're a feather in my arms

—from "A You're Adorable," *Sounds Jubilee*

Once you and the children recognize familiar cultural sequence
as the organizing factor in putting certain stories together,
you may wish to begin a bulletin-board collection
of such sequences.
And don't be surprised if the children list the count-down
as a sequence which is securely deposited
in their linguistic storehouses.

E) Chronological Sequence

Sometimes it is easy to hunch early in a story
that the episodes are arranged chronologically.
This kind of hunch gives the expectation
that the vocabulary will be influenced
by an ordering of events based on time.
Biographies and autobiographies
tend to work this way.
Very often detective stories
unfold in a time sequence.
Even in the old nursery rhyme when

Jack and Jill went ***up*** *the hill*

you expect them to come tumbling *down*.

Children are in the mood
for spanning the events of a lifetime
when they read:

This is Johnny.
He is a baby.
He cannot walk.
He cannot talk.
But he can cry!
Johnny is 1 week old.

Now Johnny can walk.
He laughs and claps his hands.
He says "dada" and "mama"
and "baby."
Johnny is 1 year old.

Now Johnny is 4 years old. . . .

He is not a baby anymore. . . .

Johnny is 6 years old now

He is in the first grade. . . .

Now Johnny is 12.

He goes to junior high school. . . .

—from "Growing Up, Growing Older,"
Sounds of Laughter

As children follow Johnny's life
through to his happy grandfather days,
they anticipate and soon are comfortable with lifetime words
such as *junior high school, young man, college,
home from the air force, wedding day.*
Even as they study the art for clues,
children have strong notions of what they are looking for
(such as signs of physical aging, and signs of maturity)
because of their recognition
of the chronological sequence on which the story hangs.

In even wider ranging applications
of this particular literary know-how,
children will create useful expectations
based on other kinds of chronological sequencing:

1) the logical ordering of events in a story,
   particularly a mystery story where the solution
   usually comes at the end:
   such as "The Ghostly Hitchhiker,"
   Sounds Freedomring

2) the ordering of events on a trip,
   be it a spaceflight or a picnic,
   i.e. "Spaceship Bifrost," *Sounds of a Distant Drum*

3) the shaping of events by weather patterns,
   i.e. "Snowbound," *Sounds of a Distant Drum*

4) explanatory sequences such as giving directions,
   i.e. "How to Brush Your Teeth," *Sounds of a Young Hunter*

F) Problem-Centered Sequence

The minute Mother Meadowlark awakens
with a snake curled about her nest,
there is no doubting that she has a problem.[5]
Whenever a main character in a story
is confronted with a crucial problem,
the person reading the story can predict
that one episode after another will occur
until the problem is solved.
Once the problem is solved
the reader does not expect the story to go on
for fifty more pages.
He knows that the story is finished.
There isn't that much more to talk about.
The episodes which occur in solving the problem
can be repetitive, cumulative,
interlocking or chronological.
They can also be arranged
around familiar cultural sequences.
In other words,
a story does not have only a basic shape.
It can also have shapes within shapes.
Children reading "The Billy Goats Gruff"[6]
soon recognize that the episodes which occur as the three goats
solve their problem with the troll
are repetitive.

[5] "Mother Meadowlark and Brother Snake," *Sounds of the Storyteller*
[6] *Sounds of Laughter*

The bridge goes,

"Trip, Trap! Trip, Trap! Trip, Trap!"

each time a goat crosses over.
The troll threatens each time.
The goats respond.
When the third goat breaks the repetitive pattern
and solves the problem,
the story comes to an end.
In their reading of the story,
children have two kinds of structural insight going for them:

1) the problem of the troll and its solution;

2) the repetition of action
and vocabulary from episode to episode.

In "The Web of Winter"[7]
the main character encounters a problem
when he discovers a young duck unable to fly
because it is frozen in the ice.
From that point on, the episodes move chronologically.
As Bill frantically tries to free the bird
and the day moves toward night,
the children reading the story
are reaching out toward a solution.
And while the problem-centered, chronological structure
does not predict the exact language,
it does prepare the children to expect vocabulary
related to the efforts to save the duck,
to the actual saving of the duck,
to the passing time of day,
to the vocabulary associated with the passing time of day,
such as *suppertime, darkness, headlights*, etc.
and to certain character traits.
All of these linguistic insights
are germane to unlocking the print.

[7] *Sounds of Mystery*

G) Rhyme-Rhythm Sequence

Some poems and stories
are put together with a dependable rhyme-rhythm scheme.

The Owl and the Pussy-cat went to sea
In a beautiful pea-green boat:
They took some honey, and plenty of money
Wrapped up in a five-pound note.

—from "The Owl and the Pussy Cat," *Sounds After Dark*

You may have been taught
that this is an A-B-C-B rhyme-rhythm scheme,
meaning that the second and fourth lines rhyme
and the rhythm is predictable.
Heaven forbid that we lecture children
about the A-B-C-B rhyme-rhythm scheme!
But we can help them verbalize the fact
that when you have figured out
the author's rhyming-meter plan,
it is easier to read the rhyming words
and to syllabicate certain words
used in the rhyme-rhythm slots.

Slowly ticks the big clock;

Tick-tock, Tick-tock!

But Cuckoo clock ticks double quick;

Tick-a-tock-a, tick-a-tock-a,
Tick-a-tock-a,☐ [8]

Do you find yourself supplying the word *tick*
to keep the rhyme scheme going?
This is how it is with response to rhyme scheme.

[8] "The Big Clock," *Sounds Around the Clock*

One way to help children verbalize
how useful a rhyme scheme can be
in recognizing vocabulary
is to read them a regularly patterned verse
and ask them to supply words you leave out.

> Boys and girls, supposing you keep your books closed
> while I read you an old rhyme.
> I'm going to leave out some of the words
> and you see if you can say those words
> even though you've never heard the poem:

This is the story

Of Susie Moriar.

It started one night

As she sat by the ☐

The fire was so hot,

Susie jumped in a ☐

The pot was so black,

Susie dropped in a ☐

The crack was so narrow,

Susie climbed on a wheel ☐

The wheelbarrow was so low,

Susie fell in the ☐

The snow was so white,

Susie stayed there all ☐

The night was so long,

Susie sang a ☐

—from "Susie Moriar," *Sounds of Laughter*

As the children supply the missing words,
they are responding to both the rhythmical and rhyming patterns
of this old jingle.
It is important to help them verbalize
their ways of figuring out the missing words
and to discuss the fact that
in their independent reading,
they can use this kind of structural insight
to figure out certain unknown vocabulary.
At some point in the discussion,
it can be useful to suggest:

> *Children, supposing you wanted*
> *to change the poem about Susie Moriar.*
> *Let's see where we can go with*
>
> *"This is the story of Jennie McGoo.*
> *It started one night as she . . ."*

As the children pick up the aa-bb-cc, etc. scheme
of the original jingle
they may be suggesting:

> *This is the story of Jennie McGoo.*
> *It started one night as she went to the zoo.*
> *The zoo was so bright,*
> *Jennie stayed there all night . . .*

Some children, however, may not respond
to the rhythm-rhyme scheme of the original jingle
and may come up with something like

> *This is the story of Jennie McGoo.*
> *It started one night as she went to sleep.*

When such a suggestion is made,
your role is to accept it positively
and help the children see the difference
between this and the original pattern.

Isn't this interesting, boys and girls?
Chuck has suggested a pattern
that doesn't rhyme the way the original poem did.
Let's follow Chuck's lead for awhile
and see where we go.

"This is the story of Jennie McGoo.
It started one night as she fell asleep.
Next thing she knew she was floating on a cloud . . ."

And so develops an innovation
that is patterned on story ideas
rather than the original rhyme scheme.
Both kinds of innovating are important.
As the children discuss differences
between rhyming and non-rhyming patterns,
they will further appreciate how recognition
of a rhythm-rhyme scheme
helps a person unlock unknown vocabulary.

Obviously there are other and more subtle literary structures
such as a story like "Old Lucy Lindy"[9]
and "Yallery Brown"[10]
in which the episodes hang on character development
but for purposes of this discussion
we have confined ourselves to those story patterns
which are most productive
in helping children predict language
and thereby unlock vocabulary.

In all of this discussion
of ways for putting stories and poems together,
we have been faced with the interesting fact
that whenever many of anything come together,
be they objects or events or words or people,
they either fall together helter-skelter
or they fall into an arrangement of some kind.
An earthquake produces hit-and-miss.
Language, whatever else, creates order.

[9] *Sounds of the Storyteller*
[10] *Sounds Freedomring*

48 TE Figuring Out How Stories and Poems Work

When children are helped to verbalize
their recognition of the various ways
authors can arrange episodes in a story or poem,
they develop a reading skill
that forever lifts them out of the
little-steps-for-little-feet way of viewing a book.
A book or story or poem, whatever else it is,
is not a succession of isolated words
to be sounded out
or an unmanageable succession
of disassociated thoughts and events.
Traditional "basic" reading and language instructions
are not "basic" in the least
unless they include opportunities
for children to develop their naturalistic and intuitive skills
in unlocking the flow of language
in its basic cultural patterns.
It's as important for a child to know
how a piece of writing is unfolding
as it is for him to know
how a word unlocks.
The joyful fact is
that as a child takes root and strength
in his abilities to anticipate literary structure,
he, simultaneously, is developing word-unlocking skills
that save him from being stranded
with "sounding out" as the only way
to manage unknown words.

5 HELPING CHILDREN VERBALIZE THEIR INTUITIVE LITERARY INSIGHTS

You may be wondering
how to help children
verbalize their structural insights.
Actually, your discussion with the children
occurs all along the line.

If the children quickly chime in
during your first reading of a story,
you may wish to engage them in easy conversation
about their ease in chiming in.

> *How come you children were able to read*
> *so much of that story*
> *without hearing it first?*

Their homely explanations will tell you
whether or not they are using
the structure of the story
as one of their ways for unlocking print.

> *When he said, "I'm not as big as a goat"*
> *and "I'm not as big as a horse,"*
> *I knew he was going to keep on saying*
> *"I'm not as big as a . . . . ."*

This is a young child's natural way for telling you
that he is beginning to recognize repetitive sequence.

> *How does it happen you children*
> *read that word* Wednesday *so easily?*

> *"Well, when the author said*
> *'On Monday I build . . .' and*
> *then when he said, 'On Tuesday*
> *I build . . .' I knew he was going*
> *to say, 'On Wednesday . . .' "*

Here a child is verbalizing his awareness
of structure built on familiar cultural sequences.

> *Isn't it interesting, children,*
> *when you figure out how an*
> *author put his story together,*
> *it helps you in your reading.*

This kind of remark will help children
generalize their experience in the use of literary structure
to unlock print.
It also helps give them the vocabulary
for verbalizing what they have experienced.
A word of caution:
generalizing statements of this kind do not come
before the children have had the experience
of successfully using story or poem structure
to make their reading easier.
If the generalizations are to be the children's—
and they must be the children's
if they are to become part
of their personal collection
of word-unlocking skills—
they must grow out of first-hand experiences.
When they do grow out of first-hand experiences,
the children will claim the generalizations as their own,
depositing them in their linguistic storehouses
for future reference.
If the children are reading independently
and can recognize words
with or without help from literary structure,
you may wish to come at your questioning
from a different angle.

> *Children, supposing you had never seen*
> *the word Wednesday (or any other word*
> *that can be anticipated*
> *by knowing the structural sequence of the story).*
> *Is there anything in this story*
> *that gives you a hint*
> *that could help you read the word?*

This kind of questioning may lead
to a full-blown inquiry
into the various ways stories and poems are put together.
The children may wish to collect and categorize
favorite stories and poems they have read in the past:
repetitive, cumulative, interlocking, familiar cultural sequences,
problem-centered, rhythm-rhyme scheme.
All of this activity should have the zestful spirit
of scientific inquiry.
The children's satisfaction will come
from really figuring out
how something in their world works.

If you are teaching older boys and girls
who have never had experiences
with this approach to word-unlocking,
you may wish to get hold of a set of *Instant Readers.*[11]
These Bill Martin books are written
around the basic literary structures
and the books are discussed from this point of view
in the Teachers Guide.
Because the books are short and the structures are exaggerated,
the children can analyze them more easily
than they can longer stories.
You can also use the earlier *Sounds of Language* readers
with older boys and girls
if you reassure them
that you are doing grown-up things with the books.
Once you get into analyzing the author's plan
for putting his story together,
the children will respect the use of the younger books.

[11] Holt, Rinehart and Winston Inc.

And don't forget to browse through
the *Sounds of Language* books provided
for your particular class.
In even the seventh and eighth grade anthologies
you will find numerous short selections
that lend themselves to obvious literary analysis.

You may have to remind yourself
that these books do not have to be read
page-by-page from cover to cover
as most other readers do.
You can pick and choose from anywhere in the book,
depending on the interests and purposes
of the children and yourself.
Neither do the selections have to be exploited
in a single lesson and then left as "finished."
You can return to favorite selections
dozens of times throughout the year
for different purposes.

> *Boys and girls, do you remember*
> *the story "Ming and Ling"* [12]
> *that we enjoyed so much?*
> *Let's take another look at it. This time . . .*

Who knows how many useful excursions
children can conduct
through a story or poem that has been deposited
in their linguistic storehouses.
This is the reason for depositing the literature—
to make it available for a lifetime
of analysis and pleasure.

[12] *Sounds Freedomring*

Some of the best opportunities
for analyzing literary structure will come
when the children are borrowing the author's pattern
and hanging their thoughts and vocabulary on it.

Boys and girls, let's take a look
at this rather simple story:

"I am not as big as a goat.
A goat is bigger than I am.

I am not as big as a horse.
A horse is bigger than I am.

I am not as big as an elephant.
An elephant is bigger than I am.

I am not as big as a whale.
A whale is bigger than I am.

I am not as big as a dinosaur.
A dinosaur is the biggest thing I know."

—from "What Is Big?" *Sounds of Numbers*

If you were to borrow
the author's exact pattern
and make your own story out of it,
what would be important to remember?
Do you think you can make
even a simple pattern like this
interesting to fourth graders?

The children will probably verbalize
that the author has a plan for repeating.
They will probably notice that the describing word *big*
is central to the language pattern.
They may comment on his way for breaking the pattern
to bring the story to a close.
They may comment that the creatures
keep growing larger.
Fourth graders have been known
to come up with innovations
on even simple structures
that give them pleasure.

I am not as bony as my sister.
My sister is bonier than I am.

I am not as bony as a fish.
A fish is bonier than I am.

I am not as bony as spareribs.
Spareribs are bonier than I am.

I am not as bony as a skeleton.
A skeleton is the boniest thing I know.

—from a fourth grader, Corbett School, Tucson, Arizona

A sixth grader chooses the pattern from "A Turkey Speaks"
in *Sounds of a Distant Drum* for his innovation.

Taco Speaks

I have never understood
why anyone would
   roast the shell
   buy the meat
   chip the pickles
   chop the lettuce
when they could
sit back
and call. . . . .

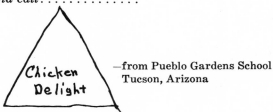

—from Pueblo Gardens School
Tucson, Arizona

Gradually you can help the children generalize
that when they are reading on their own
it is a good idea to be curious
about how the author put his story together
and that once they get the *aha!* feeling,
meaning that they have caught on to his plan,
they will be partly prepared for the vocabulary
they will encounter,
and that their structural insight
is both a writing and a reading skill.

6 FIGURING OUT HOW SENTENCES WORK

In the same sense
that a story has a shape
and a poem has a shape,
so does a sentence have a shape.
A speaker pauses, intones, gestures
to show how the words group together
and thereby reveal his meanings.
A writer uses punctuation
to help the reader see
how the words group together.

The concept of *shapes of sentences*
is somewhat implied
in our earlier discussion of *chunks of meaning*.
In speaking and writing,
words do not simply follow one another
in unrelated separateness.
They cluster together to form a chunk of meaning
and these chunks of meaning
are basic to the shape of a sentence.
Not only that.
These chunks of meaning within a sentence
do not simply follow one another in random style.
They form a pattern as they fall next to one another
and recognizing the pattern is helpful in decoding.
One additional facet in the shaping of a sentence
is the fact that there is a definite order
in which many individual words fall in English sentences.
A chunk of meaning about a pretty girl
will not reverse this culturally established order
and call her a *girl pretty*.

Let's take a closer look
at these three characteristics
that influence the shapes of sentences
and see what the implications are
for developing reading skills
that are not provided for in most reading programs.

A) Sentences Work in Chunks of Meaning

One useful way to help children understand
that chunks of meaning
are basic to the shape of a sentence,
is to read aloud a sentence from a familiar story
and ask the children to keep their books closed
and raise their hands each time
they hear a chunk of meaning:

So the little squeegy bug

followed Creepy the Caterpillar
to his home under the cattail leaf,
and soon was safe and warm,
away from the storm,
and he slept soundly
until morning.

—from "Little Squeegy Bug," *Sounds After Dark*

Remind the children that different people may hear
different chunks of meaning
so they will not be worried about right and wrong answers
when they enter into a later discussion
of where the various chunks begin and end.

At no time should a child feel embarrassed
over his selection of a chunk of meaning.
Even if he errs,
he will self-correct (the hallmark of an educated person)
when he becomes comfortable with this concept.
And by the way, if you should find yourself
selecting different chunks of meaning
from the ones we have indicated
in the sentence from "The Little Squeegy Bug,"
don't become alarmed.
Frequently more than one choice is possible.
The test is: *Does the selection of a particular chunk of meaning
have integrity in and of itself,
and does it leave a complete chunk on either side of it?*

Another useful way to help children latch on
to the chunks-of-meaning concept
is to compare the line-by-line text of a story
which is arranged in chunks of meaning
in a *Sounds of Language* reader
with a chapter in their social studies book or other textbook
where traditional paragraphing style is used
to shape sentences to rigid right-left hand margins
regardless of chunks of meaning.
On the opposite page is a pictorial comparison
of language in paragraph form
with language in chunks of meaning.
Which more readily invites your reading interest?
Since a chunk of meaning is a unit of sense,
the children may profit from discussing
whether or not breaking the sentences into units of sense
makes for more reader ease and understanding.
Accept any observations the children care to make.
Some children may be so accustomed
to the rigid right-left hand margins
that they actually find this newer page design more difficult at first.
Whatever their reactions,
this kind of comparing and free discussion
will further their understanding of the fact
that sentences work in chunks of meaning.

BLIZZARD HITS WESTERN STATES

AIR FORCE'S "OPERATION FEEDLIFT" BALKED BY CONTINUING BLIZZARD

CHICAGO, Jan. 20—One of the worst storms in memory hit Montana, eastern Washington, Utah, Nevada, Wyoming, Colorado and the Dakotas today in the form of blizzards, floods and bitter Arctic cold.

Some areas were buried under as much as 80 inches of snow, which forced the closing of schools and blocked highways. Freezing winds blew roofs off buildings, smashed windows and ripped down power and telephone lines. Brief gusts of the blizzard winds reached speeds as high as 95 miles an hour in parts of Montana and the Dakotas.

CHICAGO, Jan. 20—
One of the worst storms in memory
hit Montana,
eastern Washington,
Utah,
Nevada,
Wyoming,
Colorado
and the Dakotas today
in the form of blizzards,
floods
and bitter Arctic cold.

Some areas were buried
under as much as
80 inches of snow,
which forced
the closing of schools
and blocked highways.
Freezing winds
blew roofs off buildings,
smashed windows
and ripped down
power and telephone lines.
Brief gusts of the blizzard winds
reached speeds
as high as
95 miles an hour
in parts of Montana
and the Dakotas.

—from *Sounds of a Distant Drum*

At some point in your figuring out how sentences work,
you will want to invite the children
to take a paragraph from a story or article
that is printed with the traditional right-hand margin
and break the sentences into chunks of meaning.
The markings may vary from child to child
but no marking should violate a unit of sense.
When variations do occur,
be sure to discuss the children's reasoning
back of their choices
to determine whether or not
a child is sensing the meaning
back of the clustering of words he has selected.

Somewhere during your discussion of ways
for breaking the rigid right-hand material
into chunks of meaning,
you will want to help the children verbalize the fact
that once they are able to break unbroken sentences
into chunks of meaning,
they are developing a skill
that will stand them in good stead
in their independent reading.
Gradually they will build the habit
of seeing chunks of meaning
whether or not the text has been printed that way.
This is germane to dealing
with the meaning encased in print.

You may wish to consider punctuation
while you are discussing chunks of meaning.
As a matter of fact,
this may be the first time
some of your children see the actual sense to punctuation.
They may have seen commas and periods
and all the rest
primarily as items to get right or wrong
as they fill in blanks in workbooks.
Now with this new look at the ways sentences work,
they may enjoy discussing
how punctuation came to be in the first place.

When man invented the code
that we call written language,
he immediately found the need
for additional inventions besides the letters
to make writing work.
He therefore invented periods and commas
and other signals
to help the reader hear
what the code was saying.
Won't it be interesting
if the children decide
that printing sentences
in chunks of meaning
can make
certain punctuation
unnecessary!

The pickety fence

The pickety fence
Give it a lick it's
The pickety fence
Give it a lick it's
A clickety fence
Give it a lick it's
A lickety fence
Give it a lick
Give it a lick
Give it a lick
With a rickety stick
Pickety
Pickety
Pickety
Pick

—by David McCord,
from *Sounds of a Young Hunter*

SOX SONG
RED SOX
BLUE SOX
WHITE SOX
GREEN SOX
BROWN SOX
BLACK SOX
COLORS·IN·BETWEEN SOX

—from *Sounds After Dark*

B) Sentences Work Because of WORD ORDER

One other characteristic of English sentences,
is the *order* in which individual words
are placed next to one another.
A three-year-old knows this.
He will say:

> *Me hit you.*

It is true he is using
the incorrect form of the pronoun,
but he will not ruin the basic shape
of the sentence and say:

> *Hit me you.*

He will not rearrange the usual word-order
and put the verb in front of the subject pronoun.
He will say

> *big boy*

He will not say

> *boy big*

He will not deny the fact
that in the English language
the adjective usually comes in front of the noun.
As a school child,
if he is helped to experiment with sentences
and to verbalize his intuitive knowledge
about word-order in English sentences,
he will partially unlock words
because of where they fall
and what function they perform in the sentence.
That child coming to this sentence, for example,

I found six spotted puppies.

will not sit and endlessly spit and sputter
over the *sp* sound in *spotted*
and then give up in despair if he can't sound out the word.

He will first of all recognize
that *spotted* is a describing word,
falling as it does, in front of *puppies*.
With this dependable structural clue,
he finds it useful to know that the word begins
with the *sp* sounds.
Knowing that the word describes *puppies*
narrows the range, as it were,
to the short array of culturally anticipated words
such as:

> *little puppies*
> *white puppies*
> *black puppies*
> *tiny puppies*
> *collie puppies*
> *friendly puppies*
> *hungry puppies*
> *spotted puppies*

Instead of being confronted with the whole wide world
of words at random
he now is seeking only an *sp* word that can appropriately
describe *puppies*,

> *spotted puppies.*

What a difference in psychological posture!
What a cultural reliability
that supports a child's best efforts!

In a different context,
a writer sometimes distorts natural *word order*
for emphasis on rhythm or dramatic effect
as Walter de la Mare does in this amazing sentence:

> All but blind
>> In his chambered hole
> Gropes for worms
>> The four-clawed Mole.
>
> —from "All But Blind," *Sounds of Mystery*

C) Sentences Work in Sequence Patterns

Another characteristic of English sentences
is the way in which
the various chunks of meaning
are connected with one another.
Interestingly enough,
these clusters of words
pattern in much the same way
that the episodes in a story pattern.

1) Repetitive Sequence

Over in the meadow

in the sand

in the sun

Lived an old mother turtle and her little turtle one.

—from "Over in the Meadow," *Sounds of a Powwow*

Repetition of chunks of meaning
is central to the shape
of this sentence.
Leave out *in the sand* and *in the sun*
and the basic design of the sentence
has been altered.
Once the basic designs for arranging sentences
have been deposited in the children's linguistic storehouses,
they own them for a lifetime of transforming
in their speaking and reading and writing.

2) Cumulative Sequence

Sometimes the chunks of meaning in a sentence
just keep adding on to one another
to give the sentence its shape.

Then, each monkey pulled off his cap . . .

and all the yellow caps . . .

and all the blue caps . . .

and all the red caps . . .

and all the polkadot caps . . .

came flying d o w n o u t of the tree.

—from "Caps for Sale," *Sounds of a Powwow*

Young children are great at writing cumulative sentences
once they discover the power in the little word *and*.
You've seen these sentences:

I went home from school
and then I . . .
and then I . . .
and then I . . .
and then I . . .

Instead of criticizing the children
in our well-intentioned effort
to get them to write more interesting sentences,
we should praise them for their discovery.

Julie, that's just about the longest sentence
I ever saw.
Did you know that all of your life
you'll be seeing and hearing sentences that are put
together that way? Let's take a look at your long sentence
and see if we can figure out how it goes together.
How did it get to be so long?

Accept any homely observations
the children care to make.

Well, I just kept saying
"and then, and then, and then . . ."

is a beginning verbalization
of the shape of a cumulative sentence.

If the children made observations
about the cumulative sequencing
from episode to episode in "The House that Jack Built,"
they may enjoy going back to the story now:

This is the COCK that crowed in the morn,

That waked the priest all shaven and shorn,

That married the man all tattered and torn,

That kissed the maiden all forlorn,

That milked the cow

    with the crumpled horn,

That tossed the dog, that worried the cat,

That killed the rat, That ate the malt,

That lay in the house that Jack built.

—from *Sounds Around the Clock*

66 TE Figuring Out How Sentences Work

Imagine what fun it will be to discover
that each new episode is actually a cumulative sentence.

In your discussion of the various ways
chunks of meaning are laid next to one another
in a sentence,
don't press for exact terminology.
Older boys and girls may enjoy some terminology
after they have explored the shapes of sentences (and stories)
but the most important part of the explorations
is their homely verbalizing of their self-selected observations
about the ways in which sentences work.

3) Interlocking Sequence

> "Oh!" said Sallie,
>   and this time it was so low,
>   one could scarcely hear it,
>   for she was remembering
>   the cabbage stalk
>   and that she had seen Diccon
>   over her left shoulder.
>
> —from "Tomson's Halloween," *Sounds of a Young Hunter*

Sometimes the chunks of meaning in sentences
do not simply repeat or add on.
They interlock with one another
(as the chunks do in the sample sentence here)
in ways that create the sentence form and meaning.
For the most part,
an interlocked sentence does not reveal its full meaning
until the last segment in the chain of interlocking.

Consider, for example,
how incomplete the meaning of the following sentence is
until the last segment hinges in:

To the Sun
Who has shone
All day,
To the Moon
Who has gone
Away,
To the milk-white,
Lily-white Star
A fond goodnight
Wherever you are.

—"Last Song," by James Guthrie,
Sounds of a Distant Drum

Did you notice the repetitive sequence of this sentence?
And also that the sentence maintains a simultaneous
repetitive and interlocking sequence.
Interestingly enough,
as you will observe in the two sample sentences given here,
the chunks of meaning in one
can be reordered (re-arranged) without destroying the meaning,
while in the other
the various chunks of meaning cannot be rearranged
without destroying both the shape and meaning of the sentence.
It is as if a cyclone came along
and stripped the sentence of its sense.
Of all the sentence patterns,
the interlocking sequence is perhaps the one
that best helps children understand
that sentences are not simply long strings of isolated words
hung together with a capital letter and a period.

Sentences, like stories,
are shapes within a shape.
They are chunks of meaning
which are laid next to one another
according to a design.
Recognizing the design
helps to unlock the meaning.

4) Chronological Sequence

Chronological sentences are probably the easiest
to figure out
in terms of recognizing their basic shape.
Everything moves ahead so orderly:

First, the

utside surface of your upper teeth; second, the

The same three areas of the lower teeth
need careful cleaning: 1) outside, 2)
inside, 3) biting edge.

nside surface of these teeth; third,

e grinding surfaces of the upper teeth.

—from "How to Brush Your Teeth," *Sounds of a Young Hunter*

Here's another sample:

Then he reached up
to make sure that they were straight—
first his own striped cap,
then the four yellow caps,
then the four blue caps,
then the four red caps,
then on the very top the four polkadot caps.

—from "Caps for Sale," *Sounds of a Powwow*

And still another which is nonetheless chronological
because the time sequence is less obvious.

So she (the Grandmarina)
took it (the Magic Fishbone)
from the hand of Princess Alicia
and waved her magic fan over it,
and it instantly flew
down the throat
of the dreadful little
snapping pug dog next door
and nearly choked him,
and that was good!

—from "The Magic Fishbone," *Sounds of a Young Hunter*

Once children sense that a sentence is moving forward
in chronological sequence,
they join right in with the author (anticipate)
in planning how the chunks of meaning will be arranged.

This kind of feeling that it is possible
to work one's way through a complicated looking sentence
because of recognizing its structure,
develops into a highly useful work-unlocking skill.

5) Rhyme-Rhythm Sequence

> You can take a tub with a rub and a scrub
> > in a two-foot tank of TIN,
> You can stand and look at the whirling brook
> > and think about jumping IN;
> You can chatter and shake in the cold black lake,
> > but the kind of bath for ME,
> Is to take a dip from the side of a ship,
> > in the trough of the rolling SEA.

> —from "The Kind of a Bath for Me,"
> *Sounds of the Storyteller*

This sentence moves forward
with a rhyme-rhythm sequence that helps give it its shape.
Children will readily recognize
that the intrigue and charm of the sentence
stem equally from the rhyme—
both internal and terminal— and from the rhythm.

In the following example, however,
it is the anticipation of rhyme, not rhythm,
that focuses the sentence sequence
and the unlocking of the word *precisely.*

> . . . putting it my way, but nicely,
> > You are precisely my cup of tea!

> —from "Getting to Know You," *Sounds of the Storyteller*

Here again, it's rhythm, not rhyme, that shapes a sentence:

N ow, pray, where are you going?"
                    said Meet-on-the-Road.
"To school, sir, to school, sir,"
                    said Child-as-it-Stood.

—from "Meet on the Road," *Sounds After Dark*

Here is another sentence
so rhythmically shaped
that it stands alone like a poem:

O NCE IN THE GOLDEN TIME
    when an Irish king sat in every province
    and plenty covered the land,
there lived in Connaught
a grand old king with one daughter.

—from "The Princess and the Vagabond,"
Sounds of a Distant Drum

By clapping the rhythm of these sentences
and others that appeal,
children can develop sensitivity
to the rhythm of language,
a skill absolutely essential to anyone
who is to make a go of writing and reading.
You can, for example, invite someone to clap out a page of print
that all of the class has read frequently
to see if the selection can be recognized
solely by the linguistic rhythm.
At the same time
the children will be developing syllabication skills
in a far more functional setting
than looking a word up in a dictionary
for its stressed and unstressed patterns.

By clapping (and dancing) the rhythm of a sentence:

> I hoe and I plow
> I plow and I hoe
> And the wind drives over the main.
>
> I mow and I plant
> I plant and I mow
> While the sun burns hot on the plain.
>
> —from "Farmer" by Liberty Hyde Bailey,
> *Sounds After Dark*

the children will be getting the language
into their muscles as well as their minds,
a childhod naturality that makes language learning
pleasant and easy
until the pedants take over and deny children the use
of their basic language learning equipment.

Obviously there are other basic shapes to sentences
than the ones suggested in this essay,
but our purpose in this discussion is simply to alert you
that the clusters of words within a sentence
do fall together in various patterns
and that recognition of the pattern
is an aid in word-unlocking.
You may wish to jot down a few sentences from a favorite story
and see what observations you can make
about the patterns into which
the clusters of words fall.
First divide the sentences into their chunks of meaning
as we have done on these pages.
Then you are on your own.
Far more important than labeling the various shapes
is the recognition that sentences are not strings of words
which happen to fall together.

7 INNOVATING ON SENTENCE PATTERNS

By now you know
that when you read aloud to children
you are depositing various sentence patterns
in the children's linguistic storehouses
for a lifetime of use.
You probably are also aware
that when the children chime in on the reading,
especially in alive and dramatic ways
that include bodily movement,
they are themselves claiming and depositing these patterns.
One further activity
to help make these basic sentence structures
easily available to children for word-unlocking
in their reading and for writing and speaking,
is to invite them into systematic
and at the same time creative and lively experimenting
with the various patterns.
Here are four sentence manipulations
which have proved especially useful
for this kind of experimentation.

A) Transforming Sentences

Transforming a sentence
is the act of using the exact structure of a sentence
as the basis for creating a semantically new sentence
through either word-by-word substitution
or substitution of whole clusters of words.

> I   never   saw   a   purple   cow.
>
> —from *Sounds of Numbers*

Your first step in helping children transform this sentence,
after all of you have enjoyed reading the whole poem
from which it came,
is to copy the model sentence on the chalkboard,
leaving space between each word.
Then your conversation goes something like this:

> *Children, I'm going to draw a line*
> *to the word* cow.
> *Now, supposing we didn't want*
> *to use the word* cow.
> *What other words could we use*
> *instead of* cow?

Suggestions will begin to flow.

> I   never   saw   a   purple   cow.
> 　　　　　　　　　　　　　　　　┌ horse
> 　　　　　　　　　　　　　　　　│ pig
> 　　　　　　　　　　　　　　　　└ rabbit

> *Children, all of our naming words are animals.*
> *Supposing we wanted another kind of naming word—*
> *one that would make a spooky sentence.*

> I   never   saw   a   purple   cow.
> 　　　　　　　　　　　　　　　　┌ horse
> 　　　　　　　　　　　　　　　　│ pig
> 　　　　　　　　　　　　　　　　│ rabbit
> 　　　　　　　　　　　　　　　　│ spook
> 　　　　　　　　　　　　　　　　└ vampire

Now, children, supposing we didn't want
to use the word purple?
Who else has a describing word?

Again the suggestions will flow.

I   never   saw   a   **purple**   **cow.**

brown	horse
pink	pig
hungry	rabbit
wailing	spook
	vampire

And so it goes until the children have suggested
vocabulary substitutions for all of the words.
You may wish to enter the game,
especially if the children are not having fun
with the substitutions they suggest.

Children, does anyone in this class
like silly sentences?
Well, I'm going to give you a new action word
that will really make a silly sentence.

I   never   **saw**   a   purple   cow.

kissed
loved
hugged
milked
married

Now the lid is off and the children's merriment
knows no bounds as they contemplate kissing purple vampires
and marrying pink spooks.
You may wish to invite the children

to go back to their tables
to write sentences of their choice.
At some point you may wish
to begin gentle conversation
about the word order in the sentence.

> *Isn't it interesting, children,*
> *that we don't say:*

> **I never saw a cow purple.**

> *I wonder why not.*

The children will probably suggest
that it just doesn't sound good—
meaning that their ears have already picked up
the usual word order in English sentences.
Gradually these kinds of conversations
help children add information
to their growing notions about how sentences work.
The *Sounds of Language* readers abound
in useful sentence patterns for the children to transform.
We have annotated a few of these sentences
to get you and the children started.
No attempt has been made to annotate every sentence
that lend itself to this kind of language analysis.
The peak value of the activity will come
when you and the children learn to go over a story
after enjoying it in its wholeness,
perusing it for *model sentences* rich in analysis potential.
It is your and the children's own selection
and manipulation of *model sentences*
that firmly connects the language learnings
with a child's personal use of language.
This is a qualitatively different learning experience
from that of filling in little blanks
in typical language workbooks.

Imagine what fun you and the children will have
when you select an intriguing sentence like this one
from E. B. White's *Charlotte's Web*
as a model to transform:

	He	felt	the	pleasant	rubbing	of	the	stick
The	Wilbur	liked		brisk	prodding	in	those	rain
	pig	heard		soothing	scraping	on	these	boys
	She	wanted		incessant	dripping	after	a	enemy
	man	hated		steady	yelling	under	an	goose
	witch	ignored		heavy	knocking	over		doctor
	farmer	fought		ugly	taunting	around		wheel
	They				turning			motor
	We				humming			
					throbbing			

Soon the children will be far-ranging in their choices
of serious and silly sentences offered by the framework:

They   hated   the   incessant dripping of   the   rain

The witch dreamed of a heady ride   on her broomstick

The motor made a suspicious wheezing   during the night

From time to time, you yourself will want
to suggest a vocabulary substitution
such as *skeleton, ghost, ferocious, monotonous,*
knowing that one strong, colorful word
will result in a flurry of additional substitutions.
When children become deeply involved
in transforming activities,
there's never time for each of them to read aloud
all of their self-selected sentences.

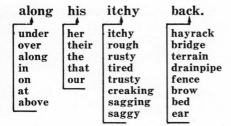

along   **his**   **itchy**   **back.**

under	her	itchy	hayrack
over	their	rough	bridge
along	the	rusty	terrain
in	that	tired	drainpipe
on	our	trusty	fence
at		creaking	brow
above		sagging	bed
		saggy	ear

through the sagging roof.

with her irritable cat.

of our scary escape.

This offers an opportunity for them to write sentences
that eventually they can read to one another.
*You can also suggest to the children
that they keep in their notebooks
a list of model sentences that especially appeal to them
for later transforming in their personal writing.*
Awarenesses of this kind
are a sound linguistic base for both reading and writing.

B) Expanding Sentences

Expanding sentences is another technique
for helping children become aware
of the shape of sentences
and for helping them develop this awareness
into reading and writing and speaking skill.
This sentence manipulation is exactly
what the term *expanding* connotes.
Any simple sentence can be expanded
by adding phrases, clauses or describing words.

Children, let's take a sentence
from our old jingle, "Susie Moriar."

This   is   the   story   of   Susie   Moriar.

Let's see if we can think of some describing words
to put in front of **Susie.**

This   is   the   story   of   Susie   Moriar.

　　　　　　　　　　　　　　　　　　　funny
　　　　　　　　　　　　　　　　　　　kind
　　　　　　　　　　　　　　　　　　　nice

Now let's think of some describing words
to put in front of **story.**

This   is   the   story   of   Susie   Moriar.

　　　　　　　　rhyming　　　　　　**funny**
　　　　　　　　silly　　　　　　　**kind**
　　　　　　　　impossible　　　　　**nice**

Now who would like to try reading a sentence
using any of the words on the board?
Have you noticed, boys and girls,
how our sentence is getting longer and longer?
There is one other way we can expand this sentence
and make it even longer.
We can add a whole collection of words
that belong together.

This	is	the	story	of	Susie	Moriar.

rhyming	funny	who lost her teeth
silly	kind	who likes to bake cakes
impossible	nice	who stands on her head

It's easy to see
that in writing the following sentence,
Anthony could have started with the simple statement:

The   king   was   old.

and then expanded it:

The King was so old
he could not dance the
twist so he said to
one of his girls to hold
him and do the twist
in slow motion.

—1st Grade, J. J. Ingalls School
Kansas City, Kansas

Older boys and girls search their linguistic storehouses
for single words and clusters of words
to make their sentence expanding worthwhile:

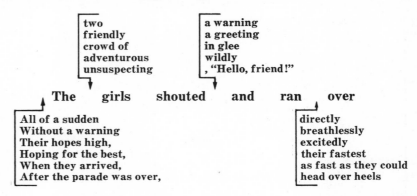

two
friendly
crowd of
adventurous
unsuspecting

a warning
a greeting
in glee
wildly
, "Hello, friend!"

The   girls   shouted   and   ran   over

All of a sudden
Without a warning
Their hopes high,
Hoping for the best,
When they arrived,
After the parade was over,

directly
breathlessly
excitedly
their fastest
as fast as they could
head over heels

An expanded sentence can be more dramatic,
"paint more pictures,"
or produce a more interesting array of sounds,
but it is not necessarily a better sentence.
In the process of expanding sentences, however,
children become keenly aware of the placement and function
of phrases and clauses and individual words
within a sentence.
And as they read their expanded sentences aloud,
they overtly are making judgments
about the kinds of sentences they do and do not like,
thus taking another step in the development of
and appreciation for a personal style
in writing and speaking.
It is this aware development
of a personal style
that helps children appreciate the fact
that authors of stories and poems
also have preferred styles.

to　Hippy Hippo's　cage .

- new
- old
- big
- open
- dilapidated
- comfortable
- air-conditioned
- well-lighted

- nearby
- in the arena
- beyond the bridge
- under the tree

—from "Hippy Hippo," *Sounds of Mystery*

A child with this kind of awareness
can browse through the first few pages
of a book he has selected from the library shelf
and make beginning judgments about the kinds of words
he will be unlocking simply by conning the author's sentence style.
If the sentences are involved
and packed with adjectives and adverbs,
this child will be sending signals to his linguistic storehouse,
as it were,
to trigger stored patterns to help with the reading ahead.

C) Transforming and Expanding Sentences

As children gain skill in sentence manipulations,
they will undoubtedly want to combine
two or more of the methods suggested here.
For example, colorful sentence possibilities emerge
when a model sentence is both transformed and expanded.
Consider the wide range of sentences
that is inherent in this diagram:

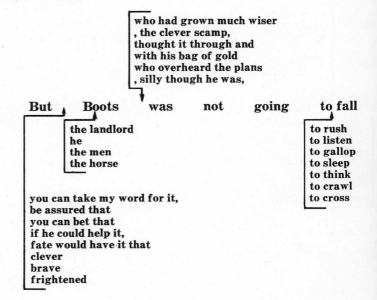

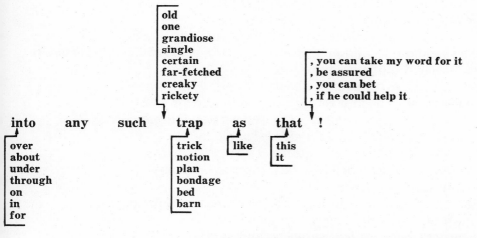

old
one
grandiose
single
certain
far-fetched
creaky
rickety

, you can take my word for it
, be assured
, you can bet
, if he could help it

into   any   such   trap   as   that   !

over
about
under
through
on
in
for

trick   like   this
notion   it
plan
bondage
bed
barn

—from "How Boots Befooled the King," *Sounds of Mystery*

Transforming and Expanding Sentences TE 85

Another sentence manipulation
that is highly useful in helping children
figure out how sentences work
is reducing sentences.
When a person reduces a sentence,
he eliminates all unnecessary words, phrases and clauses.
The danger in reducing a sentence is that one is apt
to alter or destroy the sentence meaning
or to tamper with the author's style of writing.
As you and the children go through your *Sounds of Language* readers
in search of sentences to reduce,
you may have the same difficulty we had
when we searched for sentences to annotate for you.
The sentences are generally too well written for reducing.
However, in terms of children's learning,
the search is what is important.
As they consider which words or phrases or clauses
can or can't be eliminated,
they will be experimenting with the shapes of sentences
and will be storing their learnings for later use.
Now let's reduce a few sentences and analyze the results.

A bird ~~also~~ has another way to ~~help~~ keep ~~himself~~ warm in winter.

By seeing to it that ~~the~~ birds ~~near your home~~ have plenty to eat,
you can help "keep ~~their furnaces roaring~~" ~~and~~
their bodies warm in winter.

The bird's outer feathers
~~are staggered like shingles on a roof~~
~~to~~ keep out the rain and snow.

—from "How Birds Keep Warm in Winter," *Sounds of Mystery*

In the first sentence, the reducing sharpened the sentence.
The eliminated words are truly unnecessary.

In the second sentence,
the meaning is definitely altered by the deletions.
In the third sentence,
the question is not so much whether meaning has been altered
but whether the author's style has been tampered with.
As the children read Bernard Martin's article,
they will discover that here is an author
who paints pictures in the sentences he writes.
By eliminating such a vivid picture as
(feathers) *staggered like shingles on a roof,*
the sentence is rendered unimaginative,
albeit the sentence still makes its point
that the bird's feathers keep out the rain and snow.
One useful question to ask the children
after they have reduced an author's sentence is:

> *What do you think Bernard Martin*
> *would think about his sentence now?*

If they are referring to the third sentence above,
some children will probably conclude:

> *Well, he probably wouldn't like it very much.*

Then it can be profitable to look at other sentences
that suffer from being reduced.
The children may wish to turn
to a discussion of their own preferred sentence styles:

> *Jerry, would you say that you like best*
> *to write reduced or expanded sentences?*

More than one Jerry has been known to respond:

> *Well, I really like to write reduced sentences*
> *but you're always trying to get me*
> *to write expanded sentences.*

There are no right or wrong answers to these kinds
of linguistic inquiries.
Hopefully, the children will become versatile enough
to write and read many sentence styles.

Of one thing we are certain
from our observations in research classrooms
around the country:
children who have opportunities
to experiment with the shapes of sentences
will never again view reading as a matter
of sounding out isolated words.
They will not easily bog down or stop dead in their tracks
when they come to unknown words
because they will feel the strength of the language know-how
deposited in their linguistic storehouses
both in the form of literary and linguistic patterns
and in the form of worthwhile generalizations
about how language works
which they formulate in experimentation and discussion.

E)   Rearranging Sentences

As we have already discussed,
ours is a word-order language.
The function of a word is highly dependent
on its position in the sentence.

> *I never saw a purple cow.*

A person who has listened to English sentences
all of his life, be he seven or seventy,
will hunch that the word *purple*
describes the word *cow*,
falling as it does directly in front of *cow*.
To change the word *the*
from first to second position in this sentence

> *The day is gone.*

destroys the meaning of the sentence
because the structure has been destroyed.
On the other hand,
the structure of some sentences
is not inflexible.

Jan came crying with her broken doll in hand.

can be significantly rearranged within the limitations
of our language system without a loss of meaning:

> *With her broken doll in hand, Jan came crying.*
> *Jan came, with her broken doll in hand, crying.*
> *Crying, with her broken doll in hand, came Jan.*

Let's consider the sentence patterned on internal rhyme
which we enjoyed earlier in this discussion:

1) You can take a tub

2) with a rub

3) and a scrub

4) in a two-foot tank of tin.

This sentence can be easily rearranged 2- 3- 1- 4
without destroying the structure or meaning.
You probably see other possibilities for rearranging,
while retaining the structure and meaning.
Consider the following sentence in the same light.
You readily can see multiple possibilities
for rearranging this sentence:

> A truck came bumping
> along the shore road,
> its headlights shining
> through the weeds.
>
> —from "The Web of Winter," *Sounds of Mystery*

When you work with sentences this way on the chalkboard,
be sure to invite the children to make judgments
as to which arrangement they prefer.
This is germane to developing a personal style in writing,
for it is only by putting words together
in ways that are consistent with personality
that a person develops a *style* of writing.

Rearranging sentences is one of the many structural activities
that mark *Sounds of Language* as a comprehensive linguistic program.
Unlike some linguistic programs
that focus primarily on the shape of words,
Sounds of Language accepts realistically the fact
that the sentence is the basic unit of meaning in our language
and that an understanding of sentence structure
is basic to intaking sentence meaning.

Rearranging sentences best begins
with a recognition of the clusters of words
which are arranged in a particular way
to create the basic shape of the sentence.
Once a sentence has been divided into chunks of meaning,
a useful question is:

> *Children, do you see any clusters of words in this sentence*
> *which could be moved around?*

This awareness of movable parts in a sentence
helps children in reading long and difficult sentences.
Not only do they learn to read through it one chunk at a time,
but they also learn,
if a sentence has a difficult beginning,
to start reading the sentence at an easier point
and later pick up the more difficult chunks
when they have some sentence context to help them.
In unlocking this sentence, for example,
a child who has gained skill in rearranging sentences
will not bog down on the introductory chunk of meaning
if the words are unfamiliar to him.

> Pressing his lithe body
>
> against the plastered wall,
>
> he listened
>
> and heard Nag and Nagaina
>
> whispering together
>
> outside in the moonlight.
>
> —"Rikki Tikki Tavi," *Sounds of Mystery*

Rather, he will skip down to the third chunk,
he listened,
which offers a more direct entry into the sentence.
Certain children have intuitively done this
as the natural way for making a go of a book,
until narrow reading instruction cuts them off
from this sensible, linguistically sound way
for handling complex print,
and instead teaches them to stop dead in their tracks
while they try to sound out each word
in that complicated first chunk of meaning.

Throughout *Sounds of Language* you will find
type arranged in unique and intriguing patterns—
part of our scheme to invite children
to use chunks of meaning to unlock
the linguistic puzzle.

I LOVE YOU, BIG WORLD. I wish I could call you And tell you a secret: That I love you, World... I love you, World...

by *Paul Wollner*

AGE 7

UNITED STATES

—from *Sounds of a Powwow*

8 FIGURING OUT HOW WORDS WORK

In basal reading programs and phonics programs
children spend their waking hours
considering the various ways in which words work.
In fact, in most of these programs
the word seems to be the only unit of language
worth studying.
Children learn about beginnings of words
and ends of words and middles of words.
They learn about special endings such as inflected endings.
They learn how the various letters behave in words.
And all of this they learn (or try to learn)
in line with prescriptive lesson plans
laid out in the teacher's guide.
When it is beginning consonant season,
heaven help the child who is good at looking at ends of words.
In some programs, children have to wait to beginning second grade
to even know that words have middles,
because that is when the teacher's guide
presents medial vowels.
Moreover, the methods used in teaching about words
are largely prescriptive.
Children are not invited to experiment with words
and come up with their own generalizations.
They are asked to memorize other people's generalizations
about what happens when two vowels go walking,
even though we all know that the first one does the talking
only when it feels in the mood.

You may or may not be using one of these programs
in your classroom.
Whether you do or not,
you and your children still need
the kind of spontaneous word analysis time
that is made possible with the *Sounds of Language* program.

In the same way that the children figure out
how stories and poems and sentences work
by experimenting with structures and verbalizing their discoveries,
children need to use their self-selected ways
for figuring out how words work.

Sometimes your open-ended questioning after reading a story or poem
will trigger discussions
which help children figure out how words pattern.
Supposing you have read:

One Misty, Moisty Morning

When cloudy was the weather,

I chanced to meet an old man

Clothed all in leather.

He began to compliment

And I began to grin:

"How do you do?"

And "How do you do?"

And "How do you do?" again.

—from *Sounds of Numbers*

After you and the children have thoroughly enjoyed the poem
through oral and various arrangements of choral reading
and after the children are using books
so their eyes are seeing the same patterns that their ears are hearing,
you might ask:

> *Children, what do you see interesting*
> *about those two words* misty *and* moisty?

Accept any observations the children care to make.

If Henry tells you that they both **Misty, Moisty**
have *y* at the end,
don't become ill at ease
if you are only studying beginning consonants
in your other reading program.
Some children are better at observing the ends of words
than they are at observing the beginnings of words
when they first start looking at print.
If these children learn
that nice boys don't look at the ends of words
simply because a prescriptive phonics program
is insisting on beginning sounds,
they begin to feel that there is something wrong
about them and reading
and they learn not to focus on the patterns of words
and certainly not to report their observations
if they do take a look.
How much better to praise Henry
for his accurate observation.

> *Henry, you're so great*
> *at looking at the ends of words.*
> *Perhaps you can find something else interesting*
> *about the way* misty *and* moisty *end.*

By now Henry is with you full force.
And on the heels of his success
in looking at the ends of words,
he can probably also be invited
to take a look at the beginnings of the two words.
By now some child will probably report to you,

> *Look.* **Moisty** *is bigger in the middle.*

Now the children have come face-to-face
with an interesting generalization about the ways words work.
They have beginnings and endings and middles.

ɔinggallopinggallopinggallopinggallopinggallopingg
ɪnggallopinggallopinggallopinggallopinggallopinggaɪ
ɡgallopinggallopinggallopinggallopinggallopinggallo

The generalization has meaning
because in the first place,
they were scrutinizing the printed form
of two words that entered their linguistic storehouses
through the heat and drama of read-aloud.
They are not just cold words on a workbook page.
They are words the children truly own.
The generalization also has meaning
because the children were able to sneak up on it,
as it were,
knowing it intuitively from their experiences
with oral language
and gradually verbalizing this facet
of the shape of words they are seeing in print.

One useful question
for getting this kind of discussion going is simply:

> *Children, what do you see interesting*
> *about the words on this page?*

As the children report observations
about how letters fall next to one another in words
you will have an interesting diagnostic
of who the individual children are as word-unlockers.
The child who reports seeing three words
that "all have two t's in the middle"
is telling you that he sees letter patterns in words.
The child who reports a word
"that looks just like a fish,"
may be telling you that he is one of those children
who goes into reading by seeing pictures in words
rather than spelling patterns.
How exciting!

—from a word design from *Sounds of a Young Hunter*

ggallopinggallopinggallopinggallopinggallopinggallo
allopinggallopinggallopinggallopinggallopinggallop
lopinggallopinggallopinggallopinggallopinggallopin

One productive activity
in helping primary children figure out how words work
(as well as how sentences work),
is to invite them to collect word cards
that they especially want.
This is markedly different from handing out
the same word cards to all children
with the requirement that they learn the word
as part of their basal reading program.
In this latter approach, it is the teacher who is reaching out,
trying to capture the child
and get him to learn the word selected by the teacher's guide.
When children ask for word cards of their own choosing,
they are the ones doing the reaching-out
and consequently the motivation comes from within themselves
rather than from the pressures of the outside world.
Children the nation over
demonstrated to us what they can be like
when they are invited to claim interesting words as their own.
The culture offered children the word

Supercalifragilisticexpialidocious

on the wings of a song.
We didn't tell the children they had to learn the word
before they were allowed to sing the song.
We didn't tell them that
if they were in the low reading group
we would give them a small, uninteresting word
to take the place of this complex, exciting word.
And the children responded to our freely given invitation.
It was so exciting going around the country
while "Mary Poppins" was in full swing.
The children demonstrated how they can behave
when their love of words is rewarded
by a truly worthwhile offering.
Not only could they read supercalifragilisticexpialidocious.
They could count the syllables and spell it backwards!

Words in the *Sounds of Language* reading program
are thought of as the personal possessions of each child.
At the end of reading a story or poem
you need only ask:

> *Did anyone hear a word
> you would like as your own?*

Once you give a child a word card
for each of his favorite words or phrases,
the fun begins!
Children will compare words.
They will swap with one another.
They will ask you for a blank card
to copy a friend's word.
They will arrange their word cards in patterns that

1) begin alike,
2) sound alike,
3) end alike.

They will create sentences on their desks.
Their favorite words are apt to appear
in their drawings and in their speech.

And you—think of the possibilities
for your involvement!
One bright, sunshiny morning you might announce:

> *Boys and girls,
> you'll never guess what I did last night.
> I sat up writing parts of sentences.
> When I hold one of these parts
> up in the air, if you have a word
> that will finish the sentence,
> hold it up.*

Suddenly your room will come alive
with thirty different sentences
as children hold up word cards to complete
a provocative sentence starter such as:

> *Someday I am going to kiss a* _____.

Another day you might suggest:

> *Children, do you know what let's do today?*
> *Let's put one rubber band*
> *around the word cards you do recognize*
> *and one around the words you don't.*
> *Then supposing you choose*
> *one unknown word each day*
> *to work on and change over to your known words.*

On other days the children can arrange their words alphabetically,
can group them with rubber bands
as naming words, action words, and describing words.
You can tell from this discussion,
that giving children word cards
is not the end,
but rather the beginning of a whole host
of language encounters
that help children claim the glory and workings of words.
Although it is true that filling out word cards
demands effort on your part,
you will find yourself basking in the rich rewards.
How exciting to have children ask for and value new words,
and through innate curiosity about things they value,
to analyze these words down to their most unique characteristic.
By the way, if you think alphabetizing
is the preferred way for arranging and filing word cards,
you may want to listen to your children.
Children have been known to make arrangements of

> exciting words,
> > letter writing words,
> story writing words,
> > hard words,
> easy words,
> > and even last week's words.

Interestingly enough, when children themselves
decide on methods of categorizing and filing,
they know exactly where to look for the word they need.

Those of you who teach older boys and girls
may be wondering how you can offer
the joy and productivity of word cards.
Actually, older boys and girls
have been known to do this same kind
of self-selected word collecting
with various kinds of word lists in their notebooks.
A boy who keeps a list of describing words worth using
when you want to indicate whether you're for or against a team,
is more highly motivated
than the boy who is idly writing sentences
using a list of *today's new words.*
Throughout the *Sounds of Language* program,
children are helped to analyze
the printed characteristics of words.
Surprisingly enough,
the most useful investigation
does not necessarily focus on beginnings and endings and middles.
In terms of a child's natural way for moving into print,
the first step in word analysis
is to hear and say the word orally
and count the number of syllables.
The sound of a word is its most unique characteristic
and it tends to be reflected in the printed symbol.
Let's pronounce and take a look at the word *station:*

The workmen
are going to build
a new police station here.

sta/tion

Ear and eye work comfortably together
in the word *station.*
It is easy to hear that there are two parts.
What are the useful steps to take in word analysis?

First: *"Let's listen to the word* station, *Chuck.*
How many sounds do you hear?"

Second: *"Look at the word, Chuck. (sta/tion)*
I am writing it on the chalkboard the way you say it."

Third: *"Now read the sentence in which you found the word, Chuck.*
Do you hear two sounds in station?"

Fourth: *You move from here to any next sensible step.*
It might be to look
at that intriguing tion *syllable*

"Let's look at some other two-syllable words
that look something like the word station.

sta	**tion**
na	**tion**
no	**tion**

Who knows where you go from here?
It might be to other two-syllable words
in the story, "The House Biter."
It might be to the wonderful
four-syllable word *education*
or to the intriguing *stationary*
that carries the original word *station*.

But whatever sequence you take,
you must be secure in the fact
that you can follow your own hunches
and your own common sense
in response to clues given by the children.
Children love to analyze a word they have discovered
in the context of a meaningful language pattern.
Let's not fool ourselves into believing
that there is only one sequence in word analysis.
Individual children and teachers have their own continuities
and this program invites you to respect these differences.

Then along came LITTLEFISH

9 FIGURING OUT HOW PRINT WORKS

When a child looks at a page of print,
something dynamic must happen if we hope for him to become
an intelligent, self-motivated reader.
Oh, we can force him to read as we do in many programs,
but unless he himself elects to explore the page of print
in an effort to make sense out of it,
we can safely assume
that he is not learning much about reading.
The traditional answer to this
has been simply to write stories with scaled vocabulary
so that a child's eyes will immediately see familiar words,
but there is much more
that can encourage a child to explore a page of print
than the sighting of familiar words.

You will discover that on many pages of *Sounds of Language* readers,
the type swells, lurches, screams, whispers,
undulates, turns somersaults,
and even subsides in pictorial and narrative context.

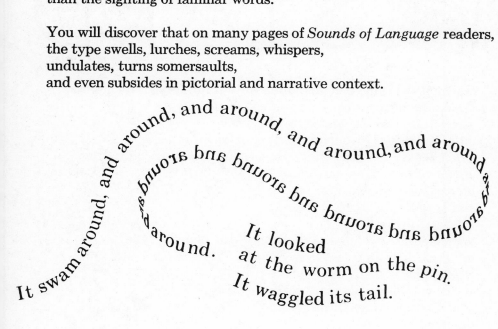

It swam around, and around, and around, and around, and around, and around, and around and around and around and around and around around. It looked at the worm on the pin. It waggled its tail.

FOOD GLORIOUS FOOD! HOT SAUSAGE & MUSTARD!

—from *Sounds of a Distant Drum*

Having type behave in intriguing ways is not foreign to children.
We adults have grown accustomed to schoolbooks
where the same size and style of type
move relentlessly from left to right, page after page,
and it is easy to forget that today's children are encountering
imaginative and flamboyant uses of type on TV,
in magazine advertising
and even on their cereal boxes.

Watch children's faces as they follow the dancing type
in *"Ten Little Indians"* from *Sounds I Remember.*
Notice how intently their eyes move with the type
and how their spirits buoy with the playful design.
In impressive ways these young children are learning
the most basic characteristic of type—
it moves from one place to another.

The sad fact is,
most of the early reading programs,
with their insistence on a rigid left-to-right
non-varying pattern of print,
actually cut children off from a fundamental cultural experience
which tells children that print is
a very versatile and exciting human invention
which to a large degree bends itself to the desires of the user.
Rules about beginning on the left and moving to the right
are not impressive invitations into the world of print.
It is a child's recognition that type moves,
a recognition that most easily comes
from pages where the movement is exaggerated,
and his determination to figure out the plan
back of the typographical puzzle
that motivate a child to make a go of reading.
Once he is caught up in the excitement
of following the movement of type as he reads,
he will himself come to the generalization
that for the most part in the English language,
type does move from left to right.

As you leaf through the *Sounds of Language* books,
you will discover that in addition to other
exciting typographical innovations,
the type generally is set in the pattern of spoken language,
just as the type in this essay
has been printed in facsimiles of oral language patterns.
Various methods have been used
to cause the reader to focus attention on selected words,
i   t relationships.
   m   n
      p   e
         o   r
            r   e
               t   h
                  a   n
                     n
                        t ideas, and i

And now for a moment of frankness . . .
When you first looked at this series of books,
did you realize that it was for purposes
of helping children figure out how print works
that the books were designed as they are?
Children are curious about how print works,
just as they were curious about how spoken language works.
The *Sounds of Language* readers reward this curiosity
by helping children relate all that they know about spoken language
as they unravel the secrets of print
and make these secrets work for them.
You will want to help the children verbalize
their adventures with print in the *Sounds of Language* readers.

Children, can you see the shapes of those words
slurpy and glurpy? Take a close look.

—from *Sounds Around the Clock*

Hey la la, Ho la, My donkey and I, Trotting to market with cheeses and pie, Trotting to market with cheeses and pie, If you should stumble, we'll never get there, Hey la la, Ho la, My donkey and I. Hey la la, Ho la, Oh Donkey take care, If you should stumble, we'll never get there, My donkey and I, We'll eat those cheeses, And we'll eat that pie, Hey la la, Ho la, If no one should buy, we'll eat those cheeses, If no one should buy.

An old song, author unknown.

painting by Vic Herman

—from *Sounds After Dark*

As the children pore over this especially designed page,
they are role-playing in exaggerated fashion
the fact that if a person studies the puzzle of a page of print
he will discover signals and patterns
that help him decode what he is encountering.

In a similar way
when a child looks at the printed page of the old song above
and says, "I know where that song begins,"
he is showing that he has found enough clues
to get a start on unravelling the puzzle.
Which clues worked for him?
Was it the capital letter? Starting on the left?
The space in the lower left-hand corner?
The actual clues he found do not matter as much as the fact
that he expects his search to be rewarded.

One indication that the children are beginning
to make typographical arrangements work for them
is their experimentation with intriguing arrangements
of words and letters and numbers in their own writing.
The more children can get the notion that written language
is an exciting and dependable puzzle
with multiple clues for the person who is reading,
the more confident and successful they will be
in their independent reading.

For the psychological advantages as well as for pure enjoyment,
from time to time write on the board
familiar sentences in reverse direction,
in scattered fields of letters,
in upright rocketing,
in straight downward plunges,
in crisscross fashion.
And even upside down and backwards.

Then watch the children delight
as they put all of their linguistic skills
into the decoding of the language.
It is dramatic experiences like these
that stand children in good stead
as they engage in the routine aspects of decoding.
Children will work at identifying initial consonants
or medial vowels or moving from left to right
with more personal determination and pleasure
when they see such activities
as part of the larger and more exciting process
of figuring out the puzzle of print.

10 DEVELOPING SKILL IN COMPREHENSION

Contrary to the view of many reading programs,
comprehension is not merely a matter
of the reader's proving that he has "read" the selection.

All too often this kind of proving simply means
listing main events, main characters, key words,
character traits, and snatches of figurative language.
Comprehension activities takes on true character
when they involve the reader or listener in such ways
that he comes to grips
with his and his colleagues' personal interpretations
in relation to the author's intended meanings.
If you care about this kind of comprehension,
much depends on the kind of questions you ask children.
For example, a question like

> *How far did John walk?*

has only one possible answer to children
who have just read that John walked six miles.
Even if a child gives the "correct" answer,
what has he actually gained from this "educative process"?
As a matter of fact, the first child who gives the answer
closes the discussion.
The "educative process" comes to a close.
There is nowhere else the discussion could possibly go.
And how smart some children are in knowing
which children in the group will give the *correct answers* first!
Many simply do not expect to participate
in unimaginative rituals of this kind,
and gladly play the role of passive observers
because the situation structures such roles.

Think, on the other hand, what happens to children
if the teacher accepts the fact
that she doesn't have to make the children prove
that they have read the story threadbare,
and, therefore, can ask intriguing comprehension questions,
such as,

> *Children, the story says John walked six miles.*
> *How far is six miles?*

Every child now—even those who read less well than others—
views himself as an active participant in the discussion
and will gladly contribute his thoughts and feelings,
knowing that the purpose is to examine and probe personal meanings.

You may want to ask yourself if your questions
are the kind that stimulate thoughtful discussions
by which each reader can evaluate the meanings
he gleaned from and brought to the story.
Nothing is more exciting, more conducive to learning,
than to participate in a cross-fire of opinions and ideas
generated by a common experience, such as story meanings.
Here are some examples of questions
that will trigger off lively discussions
that will contribute to children's comprehension of the world
in which they live:

> *How long is a person young?*

The story "Growing Up, Growing Older" says,

> *John is now a young man.*
> *He is eighteen years old.*

How easy and unrewarding it would be to ask:

> *How old was John when he was a young man?*

A child could answer *18 years old* and be correct,
but what kind of thinking,
what kind of language usage,
what kind of mental and emotional involvements
does his answer promote?

The openness of a true comprehension question invites children
to put everything they know about life
(in this case, what constitutes being young or old)
into their answer.
It also invites all children to participate in the discussion,
not only he who happens to speak first.
And make no mistake!
When you ask children how long a person is young,
you are going to get an array of life-related answers.
Many a child feels old at six,
and anyone old enough to go to college is positively antiquated.

Your comprehension questions about a story
will trigger off a whole hierarchy of meanings
ranging from gross understanding to precise verbalizing,
from a simple restatement of story meanings
to a complex conjecture about the whole realm of living.

Annotated in *Sounds of Laughter* for the consideration of both you
and the children is the question:

> *Is it hard not to speak in anger*
> *when your heart is filled with anger?*

The children have just been reading
the story of an Indian boy and his grandfather
and they have heard the grandfather advise the boy
not to speak in anger.
But the concern of the moment is not the grandfather's advice.
The concern is the feelings of the alive children in your classroom
who are encountering this advice.
We must not assume that comprehension can be measured
only in terms of "correct" answers to tight little questions.
The important thing is,
each child is pitting his own meanings against the author's
and gradually coming to know what the story means to him.
The cross-pollenation that occurs
in such discussions
also invites children to question their own meanings
and even to organize new meanings.

Here are some examples of questions
that should trigger lively discussions
that will both focus the literary experience
and contribute to children's comprehension of human behavior.

A) *Why does the author suggest that on Halloween night*
it is "just as well" to answer civilly
when one is asked a question?
"Tomson's Halloween," *Sounds of a Young Hunter*

B) *If Bill held an after-school job for which he was paid a salary,*
would he, after finding the trapped duck, have
ignored the reporting-in time, just as he did
when it was time to report in to his mother at dark?
Would you? "The Web of Winter," *Sounds of Mystery*

C) *Do you like Mr. Lincoln better with or without a beard?*
Why? "A Vote for a Beard," *Sounds of a Young Hunter*

D) *Well, children, what do you think*
of a free-wheeling literary-artistic-dramatic-boisterous
story like this?
"How Old Stormalong Captured Mocha Dick," *Sounds of a Distant Drum*

Another insightful way of getting into
a full-blown discussion of story meanings
is to ask questions that relate to the author or artist's techniques
of putting a story or a picture together.

A) *A comparison of the descriptive line in "Facts About*
Angry Bears"
with the dramatic story line in "Little Balser and the
Big Bear"
(or any other comparison of a factual article
with a story with a strong plot), for example,
will reveal much of children's understanding of the
selections,
although, ostensibly, they are discussing literary
structure.—from *Sounds of a Young Hunter*

B) *What has the artist done in this picture to convey*
    to you that this is a make-believe story?
    "Proud Peacock," *Sounds of a Young Hunter*

C) *What clues do you get from the title and the illustrations*
    as to what kind of reading you will find in this selection?
    "The Birth and Growth of a Tree," *Sounds of a Distant Drum*

Enough comprehension questions have been annotated
throughout this program
to give you the feel of framing open-ended questions
that promote a depth of comprehension and feelings of self-respect.
Once you have experienced
the dynamics of a vital group discussion,
in contrast to a boring kind of question-answer ritual,
you will be well on your way to becoming that kind of teacher
whom children remember and revere.
The art of good teaching has deep roots
in the ability to motivate meaningful discussions.
Of course, post reading discussions are not the only way
for children to organize their reading meanings.
When the fourth grade teacher reads

> Giant Thunder striding home
>
> wonders if his supper's done.
>
> *'Hag wife, Hag wife, bring me my bones!'*
>
> > *'They are not done,'* the old hag moans.
>
> *'Not done? not done?'* the giant roars
>
> and heaves his old wife out of doors.

and Bill blurts out "*Sounds just like my father!*"
it is not necessary to ask a lot of tight little questions
about who came striding home and what wasn't done.
Bill's comprehension is proved in his spontaneous response
and the laughter of his classmates
is ample proof that Bill's comprehension is shared.

When the kindergarten teacher opens to the title page
of an honest-to-goodness spooky book
and Therese promptly gets up from her place
at the teacher's feet
and moves as far away from the book as possible
while still remaining in hearing range,
there is little doubt but that Therese understands
the mood of the story.
And as the story progresses
and Therese keeps moving back and forth—
now near the book, now far away—
she is using her entire body
to express her comprehension of the story.
Six-year-old Brenda's spontaneous response to A. A. Milne's line

So I think I'll be six now for ever and ever.

—from *Sounds Around the Clock*

needs no explanation.

I do not want to be six
for ever because I want to be
a nurse because I want to help
people and a whole gob of
people will say thank you. Brenda

—1st Grade, J. J. Ingalls School, Kansas City, Kansas

Children are bubbling with spontaneous responses
to stories and poems until they learn
that there is only one thing that happens
after reading a story:
the teacher asks questions.
If your children do not seem to respond spontaneously
and you have a notion it is because
they are in this other habit of thinking about story response,
you may have to be the one in your class who responds
spontaneously to a story
in order to get the whole spontaneous,
personalized reaction-thing going.
After reading about John and his six mile walk,
for example, if you slap yourself on the thigh
and exclaim

> *WOW! What an idiot!*

and in other ways role-play the fact
that this kind of responding is a legitimate way
for showing comprehension,
the children will soon pick up the invitation
and reading time will take on more life.

And of course you are aware
that painting and dancing and creative dramatics
are also productive ways
for organizing personal meanings
brought into play by a story or poem or article.

One last thought about comprehension.
You may be interested to reread our discussion
FIGURING OUT HOW STORIES AND POEMS WORK, page 24.
And **FIGURING OUT HOW SENTENCES WORK**, page 56.
In both of these teaching strategies
are numerous suggestions
of times when the structure of a story or poem or sentence
deeply influences the meaning.
Those of us who study language in human affairs
can only conclude that structure is itself
one expression of meaning.

The post-reading discussions in *Sounds of Language*
that are triggered off by the open-ended comprehension questions
and by certain language-analysis questions

A) put each child in touch with his own thoughts and
feelings that have been generated by the reading,

B) put him in touch with the feelings and thoughts
of other children who supposedly shared an "identical"
reading experience, and

C) help him verbalize his growing insights
into the workings of language, both in oral and written
form.

The child's self-expressions, therefore, have a rare dynamic quality
as he searches for verbal ways to express the inner growth
that his reading occasioned.
Every speaking skill he employs,
everything from sentence patterns to figures of speech,
is influenced by the integrity of his speaking situation.
His *preciseness* in self-expression, therefore,
actually is preciseness in making language work to express
and thereby validate his own personality.

11 LINKING WRITING TO READING

In *Sounds of Language* children are helped
to develop writing skills
in the same naturalistic, linguistically sound ways
that they learn to read.
Just as kindergarteners and young first graders
latch on to highly structured rhymes and stories
and role-play themselves as readers,
these same young children begin innovating
on the author's pattern and role-play themselves as writers.

Hello! My name is Pamela, K.
I am a maker of costumes.
I make funny costumes and scary
costumes. These are the
costumes I make.

—2nd Grade, J. J. Ingalls School
Kansas City, Kansas

Gradually they learn to use their *Sounds of Language* books
as resource books for personal writing.
They know that these books are crammed
with story patterns and rhyme schemes and sentence patterns
that are theirs for the asking.
They also know that they have the practical know-how,
transforming sentences, for example,
for taking an author's structure
and hanging their own thoughts on it.

As one young child exultantly declared
after borrowing the literary structure
and sentence patterns of "The Billy Goats Gruff"
to successfully write his own story about three skunks
who encountered a troll on their way to eat garbage:

I only needed three new words
for my whole story—
> skunk
> *and* garbage
> *and* smelly.

I almost needed the word stinked
so I could say
the skunk stinked the troll,
but I remembered
you gave me the word skunk
and I could use that to say
the skunk skunked *him.*

—from Mueller School, second grade, Wichita, Kansas

Once children become accustomed to using their reader this way,
you will be amazed by both the quality and quantity
of their writing.
Moreover, you will have a solution to the nagging problem
of what kinds of "seat work" to provide the rest of the class
while you are busy with a few children.

12 CULTIVATING LITERARY AND ESTHETIC APPRECIATION

The content of the *Sounds of Language* readers
is specifically planned to place literary appreciation
at the heart of the reading program.
From the very first day of first grade
throughout the entire elementary school experience,
children using *Sounds of Language* readers
will be living in the midst of a gallery of contemporary art
and in a climate of literary appreciation
that sensitize their responses and imprint their memories
with high idealism and soul-stirring emotions.

Esthetic response can only be nurtured.
It cannot be taught.
By a wide and continuing exposure
to stories, poems, art, photos, and language
that possess some pretension to taste,
children will begin to know what they do and do not like.
Knowing what one does not like
is equally important as knowing what one enjoys.
Whatever else, a child's response must be self-selected,
and it must be sincere.
We teachers need to learn how to live with children's responses
which move against the grain of our own preferences
and which reveal pleasure in the mundane.
Many children, for example, will necessarily go
through a long period of literary exposure
before they are apt to sense the worthwhileness
of Emily Dickinson's poem "Autumn"
as compared to the joy they found in their favorite comics.

Be assured that those pleasurable times of the day
when you read aloud to children
are all a part of a program in literary and esthetic appreciation,
as well as a part of the reading program.

One especially productive technique
for helping children make these kinds of value judgments
comes about through an adaptation of Sidney Simon's value line
suggested in the drawing on the opposite page.
Simply list a few of the stories and/or poems and/or articles
the children have been reading
and suggest that they rate each one
by placing it in a self-selected spot
on their own copy of the value line.
In order to help the children understand
that the value line is not an instrument
for placing one selection at the low end of the line,
another at the high end,
and the rest at equal intervals along the line,
you might want to engage them in conversation
about their use of the line.
Help them understand that the value line
does not only apply to the seven stories
they are rating at this time.
The value line has places for all the stories
they have or ever will read.
The seven stories they are rating today
might all fall at the middle or top of the line.
Or they might scatter up and down the line.
You see, the value line is actually part of each of us.
It is man's way
for placing a value on things he encounters in life.
The value line might be used to rate happenings
or foods or school subjects or teachers or movies, etc.
The important thing to remember is—
there is no special ruler to measure the experiences of such stories, etc.
and to place them on the value line.
It is a person's response from his value
that places them one place or another on the value line.

Don't try to tell the children all about the line
at one sitting.
Put the line on the board
and start using it informally,

asking the children for suggestions
as to where some of the stories might fall.
As you talk together and the children differ
about certain ratings,
they will come to understand how the line works.
After a few minutes, suggest that they draw their own lines
and place the seven stories where they want them.

1) *The Red Dragon*

2) *The Power of Eye*

3) *The Grandmother Story*

4) *The Buck and the Old Man*

5) *How the Leopard Got His Spots*

6) *The First Schlmiel*

7) *Every Man Heart Lay Down*

—selections from *Sounds Jubilee*

LOW   MID   HIGH

Once the children have placed the stories somewhere on the line,
the fun begins.
Invite the children to meet as a group
to discuss their various placements.
How your classroom will ring with developing values
as the children explain and even defend
their various designations on the line!
And what a basic learning for the children
when they discover that three people can read the very same story
and come up with highly different evaluations—
all of which can be defended.
They might even deduce that if three different teachers
rather than just one gave them report card grades,
they would come up with differing marks.
What a nice blow to the righteousness of report card grades!

13 DEVELOPING SENSITIVITY TO THE THREE LEVELS OF LANGUAGE

Sounds of Language rejects the notion of "right" and "wrong"
in judging a child's language performance.
We recognize, instead, that there are three levels of language
that every child has a right
to experiment with, enjoy, and claim as his own.

A) Home-Rooted Language

The first level of language,
indigenous to the child's life itself,
is his *home-rooted (in-group) language*.
This language may or may not be grammatically correct.
It is the language he inherited from his family,
the language that is native to his soul
and sounds best to his ear.
This language may or may not feed comfortably
into the classroom,
but if we want our classrooms to be language laboratories
where a child feels free to experiment
with new linguistic patterns,
we must first of all respect the language he brings to school.
Both you and the children may be surprised to see
the number of selections in *Sounds of Language*
that are written in *home-rooted language*.
This can help both you and the children
better respect vernacular for its beauty
and for its direct communicative impact.
Isn't it fortunate that folklore
has helped us keep the richness of home-rooted language
in the bloodstream of our language heritage!

A copperhead snake made for me
one day when I was hoein' my corn.
Happened I saw him in time,
and I lit into him with the hoe.

He thrashed around,
bit the hoe-handle a couple of times,
but I fin'lly killed him.
Hung him on the fence.
Went on back to work,

—from "The Snakebit Hoe-handle," *Sounds of a Young Hunter*

For a picture of what linguistic heights
young children can reach
when their home-rooted language is respected,
see the dictated story from a young primary child
on the next page.
Obviously someone had read "The Billy Goats Gruff"
to this child, and just as obviously,
the child stored the basic structure of the story
in his linguistic storehouse.
Notice how faithful he is to the fact
that this is a story organized around a problem.
How faithful he is to the repetition in the episodes!
How faithful he is to the solving of the problem!
If the school had *made* him feel uncomfortable about his language,
he would have "dried up" and looked like one of those "children
without language"
we hear so much about.
We ourselves wonder if it is so much a matter
of "children without language"
as it is a matter of children who have been asked in effect
to check their home-rooted language outside the classroom door.

Them all going up to the grass where you eat and the mean old troll said "Who walkin' on my bridge?" I comin' up to eat you and little Billy Goat said "Don't eat me. Wait for my next brother to come.

So da troll said O.K. I will wait. So he waited and the next brother comed and the big old troll said who walkin on my bridge. Me, next billy goat Gruff. Wait don't eat me wait.

Then boomp boomp I comin up to eat you. So he did. He tossed the mean old troll up to the sky and eat him all up.

B) Public Language

The second level of language is *public language*.
This is the corps of language ways
that society uses to carry on its organized life.
It is the grammatically correct language that facilitates
broad and precise communication with the English-speaking community.
When standards of "right" and "wrong" are used
to evaluate language (heaven forbid!)
public language is the form that is said to be "right."
Public language should not be made available to children,
on the basis of "right" and "wrong,"
but rather as one of three ways to express themselves.

Different situations call for different kinds of language.
Just as public language works best in some situations,
so does home-rooted language in others.
When a child knows that he has a choice in language usage,
public language for him gains intrigue and respect.
Many articles and essays in *Sounds of Language* are written
in public language
to help children appreciate its direct, uncluttered, and practical
effectiveness.

Most of the Indian tribes
of the early American frontier
lived by hunting buffalo
and other animals.
These tribes were wanderers.
They were good hunters
and fierce warriors.

—from *Sounds of a Distant Drum*

Westfield, Chautauque Co NY
Oct 15, 1860
Hon A B Lincoln
  Dear Sir
My father has just come from
the fair and brought home
your picture and mr. Hamlin's.

—from *Sounds of a Young Hunter*

The children may be interested in discussing
why Grace Bedell chose public language
when writing her letter to Abraham Lincoln.
This can lead to a discussion
of whether certain home-rooted expressions
might be appropriate in a letter to a best friend, to a stranger.
These discussions of language choices
give children feelings of power and pleasure
about themselves as language users.

C) Life-Lifting Language

Sing hey! Sing hey!
For Christmas Day
Twine mistletoe and holly
For friendship glows
In winter snows,
And so let's all be jolly.

— an old rhyme from *Sounds of a Young Hunter*

The third level of language is *life-lifting (literary) language.*
It is any bit or unit of language,
such as a story or poem or expression,
that is so memorable that it tends
to impress itself indelibly on the mind
and thereby become part of the culture's cherished language ways.

In

December   *"Get*

autumn   *ready*

calls   *for a*

its   *winter*

warning,   *morning!"*

It has been our experience
that many children whose home-rooted language
does not open-end comfortably into the public language
take on the public forms more easily
through poetry and other literature
than they do in lessons on public language.

Peck

    peck

       peck

on the warm brown egg.

OUT comes a neck.

OUT comes a leg.

      How

         does

           a chick,

    who's not been about,

    discover the trick

    of how to get out?

—"Baby Chick" by Aileen Fisher,
Sounds of Numbers

Consider the language thrust that any child will receive
if, throughout his elementary school years,
he has such broad and continuous exposure to memorable language
that he intakes into his mind's treasury
twenty or more poems a year.
This experience in and of itself
provides a major bridge for any child
into the culture's language storehouse,
and, at the same time, fills his mind
with high idealism and humanistic feelings.
The pervasive use of choral reading and choral speaking
in *Sounds of Language* is geared to this end.

Speak gently, Spring, and make no sudden sound;

For in my windy valley, yesterday I found

New-born foxes squirming on the ground—

    Speak gently.

—from "Four Little Foxes" by Lew Sarett,
Sounds of a Storyteller

Developing Sensitivity to the Three Levels of Language

All: We sing of thee, America,
Land we love, America,
Hear our song of Liberty,
Our country 'tis of thee.

Narrator: Our country 'tis of thee we sing,
land of New England meadows and southern cottonfields,
of county fairs, and ticker-tape parades,
barefoot boys with fishing rods
and Ladies' Day at the baseball park.
    A land of steel,
and industry,
and invention
with a heart as big as Texas
and dreams as tall as the great Northwest.

All: But where did it all begin?
Who made it possible?

Narrator: Well, to start with
There was a man . . .

—from "Our Country 'Tis of Thee,"
Sounds of a Distant Drum

Moreover, the choral speaking and choral reading
that children continuously do as part of this reading program
help them develop an appetite for the life-lifting language of literature.
As children's ears begin to know the pleasures
of this kind of language and this kind of reading,
their whole disposition toward life as well as toward literature
is affected.

In developing attitudes of literary discrimination,
each child should be encouraged to keep a running list
of his five favorite stories and poems.
Whenever he wants to add a new favorite to his list,
he necessarily must decide which of his former favorites
must be removed.
Only by exercising his own judgment in these matters,
without interference by an over-anxious adult,
will he gradually refine his sensitivities to literary ways.

Paul Bunyan

A poem by Arthur S. Bourinot

Solo: HE CAME,
      STRIDING
      OVER THE MOUNTAIN,
      THE MOON SLUNG ON HIS BACK,
All: LIKE A PACK,
Solo: A GREAT PINE
      STUCK ON HIS SHOULDER
      SWAYED AS HE WALKED,
      AS HE TALKED
      TO HIS BLUE OX
      BABE;
      A HUGE, LOOMING SHADOW
      OF A MAN,
All: CLAD
      IN A MACKINAW COAT,
      HIS LOGGER'S SHIRT
      OPEN AT THE THROAT
Solo: AND THE GREAT MANE OF HAIR
All: MATCHING,
      MEETING
Solo: THE LOCKS OF NIGHT,
      THE SMOKE FROM HIS CAULDRON PIPE
      A CLOUD ON THE MOON,
All: AND HIS LAUGH
      ROLLED THROUGH THE MOUNTAINS
      LIKE THUNDER
      ON A SUMMER NIGHT
Solo: WHILE THE LIGHTNING OF HIS SMILE
All: *Split* THE HEAVENS
      ASUNDER.

—from *Sounds of a Young Hunter*

Developing Sensitivity to the Three Levels of Language TE 127

14 DEVELOPING SENSITIVITY TO HUMANNESS

Often in classroom teaching
we become so preoccupied with "skill development"
that we tend to forget that the primary purpose of teaching
is to help children claim kinship with man's humanity.
As you use the *Sounds of Language* selections
to create a spiritual setting in your classroom
that inculcates and fosters feelings of individual worth
and high idealism,
you can be assured that you are engaging
in humanly-useful language teaching and "skill development."

For it is *on the wings of words* .
that man claims his identity with his culture.
We must help children find access to those words.

Can you imagine, without giving yourself over
to a feeling of great joy and accomplishment,
what will happen to children who for six years
during their elementary school reading experiences
feel the flow and depth of life-lifting language in their daily lives?

And if the *Sounds of Language* program
fulfills all of its expectations,
you and I and every concerned human being
who has dedicated himself to helping children learn
will have developed a camaraderie
that will change the course of language instruction in our schools
and make language truly available to children
in terms of their emerging human needs.